Praise for Valerie A.

The essence of this new book on relationships is in the opening sentences - doing something 'contrary to what you truly want.'

This suggests that you inherently know what is right and good for you but for whatever reason you choose to suppress that awareness and ignore your better judgement and often with painful consequences and lasting feelings of guilt and shame.

Valerie Campbell brings a fresh and compassionate set of eyes, her qualifications and her own experience to this age-old problem with strategies for self-forgiveness and improving self-worth. Ultimately the reader will emerge with a grounded sense of self-trust and a genuine inner strength to act authentically.

Andrew Priestley Grad Dip Psych, B.Ed,
Business coach and author of 'Don't Start ... Yet!'

~~~~~~~~~~~~~~~~~~~

As women, we're used to putting on facades in public for a variety of reasons. This book gives us the reassurance that it's okay to free ourselves from the restrictions of the façade, and in turn, take charge of our lives in a proactive and truthful way. She's Got That Vibe teaches us how to attain "the vibe", and thus, flow through life effortlessly with a strong sense of personal validation coupled with self-respect. Ultimately, this book is about motivating us to bring out the best of ourselves as women, and in so doing, helps us to improve every aspect of our lives from relationships to friendships and career.

Susan Sun
Project Manager/Production Coordinator @ Rimagine
Neuroscience and Behavior BSC University of California Santa Cruz

~~~~~~~~~~~~~~~~~~

Finding Mr Right is a challenge for most of us. Indeed, being single can also be as challenging. In order to attract the right mate, some serious reflection on your inner beliefs and the signals or vibrations you send out is essential.

If you're not getting what you want, or as the case is here, who you want, it's time to stop and reflect. In this book Valerie takes you through an interesting journey of self-discovery. Her book is not only guided by extensive research but also her own personal experience. A most thought-provoking read.

Heather Katsonga-Woodward
~ Author, Founder at NenoNatural.com
Economics First Class Honours – Cambridge University

~~~~~~~~~~~~~~~~~~

She's got that vibe is essential reading for any woman who is looking for that special man but keeps missing the mark. I love the way Valerie has turned the focus from looking outside to looking within and checking on those invisible but perceptible signals you're giving out. No amount of lipstick will draw those guys to you if your vibes are signalling them to stay away.

This book goes a long way to explaining why the girl who has nothing more going for her than any other girl never seems to have any problem attracting the right kind of man.. Sending out the right vibes is definitely the strongest weapon in a girl's hunt for the right man.

Harjeet Virdee (BA, MSc International Business)
Founder Break The Bounds consultancy and training.

~~~~~~~~~~~~~~~~~~~

SHE'S GOT THAT VIBE

HOW TO ATTRACT YOUR BOO BY BEING AUTHENTICALLY YOU!

VALERIE A. CAMPBELL

She's Got That Vibe
©Valerie A. Campbell 2014
www.ShesGotThatVibe.com

Contact Details:
Valerie A. Campbell
E: **campbell_valerie@yahoo.co.uk**
F: **www.facebook.com/shesgotthatvibebook**
P: **www.pinterest.com/shesgotthatvibe/**
T: **www.twitter.com/shesgotvibe/**
B: **www.valerieacampbell.com**
w: **www.shesgotthatvibe.com**

Cover design Nik, of bookbeaver.co.uk,
Page layout by David Springer
Back Cover Photograph Peter Branch
at peterbphotos.com

First published 2014

Dedication

'For Ma, with love.'

Contents

Foreword

Dear Woman Of Vibe,

Woman Of Vibe? I hear you say... What is that? Well after reading this book you will certainly be in the know.

You have a secret power and this book shows you how to harness and use it!

She's Got That Vibe uncovers an age-old secret. So brace yourself to be enlightened.

*There is a society of women that have **'that vibe'**. The Woman Of Vibe knows how to hold a **V**ision and Intentionally **B**ring it into her **E**xperience. Upon reading this book, you will realise that, unwittingly, you have been using this power all along to both your detriment and advantage. No doubt you will feel a profound sense of well-being as you realise that you too can leverage this power to deliberately attract your ideal partner and carve out a wonderful love life.*

Want to know the real reason you are attracting Mr Wrong? How you can attract and capture the heart of your Mr Right? Perhaps how Women of Vibe are secretly doing this ...effortlessly?

You're about to discover the 'how' within the pages of this book, as you are equipped with the tools to become such a woman.

The core message is: change your vibes to change your love life!

Raymond Aaron
New York Times Best-Selling Author
Branding Small Business for Dummies
Double Your Income Doing What You Love

Raymond Aaron was one of the very few filmed for The Secret, a ground-breaking documentary, produced 2006, revealing the secret behind joy, health, money, relationships and love. It attracted high profile interest from mogul media figures such as Oprah Winfrey and Larry King.

Foreword by Marie-Claire Carlyle, Author of "How to Become a Money Magnet" and "Money Magnet Mindset"

Most people I know are looking to be happy, financially successful and in love. On paper, that doesn't sound too difficult does it? What's more, we are now being told by Quantum Physics scientists that we are the creators of our lives; that if we want something, all we need to do is get clear on what we want, create a vision board and stay open to it happening sometime soon!

My vision board was full of pictures of happy couples and yet I was still single. It wasn't until a friend pointed out that I had created a world where everyone else was in couples that I realised I had reinforced a belief that I was destined to be single in a world of couples!

Back to the drawing board...

"She's Got That Vibe!" reminded me of my own power to create the relationship of my dreams. It reminded me of who I really am and how important it is to honour my own sense of self. It made me question how much I really wanted a relationship and it helped me get clear on what type of relationship I wanted. Best of all, Valerie helped me to see all the tangible ways where I had been letting myself down.

This is a book about how much you truly value yourself. "She's Got That Vibe!" explains the theory AND gives you real practical guidance as to how you can increase your personal self-worth. You don't need a man to feel better about yourself. You need to feel better about yourself ...and the man will then find you!

Enjoy the read....then enjoy the journey to find the authentic you!

Acknowledgments

First and foremost I give thanks to The Most High, my Father and Creator for the insight and direction to write this book and dearest spirit Emily for her guidance and always being there to speak with me when needed.

I thank my dearest mother for her guidance and putting me on the path to be a strong woman, she is the strongest woman I know. Making my mother proud is important to me.

I thank my friend Delonte who has accompanied me on this daily journey, albeit via WhatsApp! ... Championing me on, always with an ear to listen. I pray for her many blessings.

I thank Raymond Aaron, author of 8 best-selling books, including *Branding Small Business For Dummies, Double Your Income Doing What You Love* and the co-author of New York Times best-seller *Chicken Soup for the Parent's Soul* who inspired and guided me in a practical way to writing this book. Special thanks to the key speakers and support team of the Key Person Of Influence program, who set me powerfully on the path to finding my purpose.

I thank the 'special men' in my life who have been my antagonists, driving me to wanting to really know what I want, what makes relationships tick and how to be both authentic and happy, all at the same time. I thank Susan my editor from AllWordsMatter.co.uk for her patience and attentiveness in the editing of this book. Also Marie-Claire Carlyle, author of *How To Become A Money Magnet* which gave me great insight into my limiting beliefs, not to mention the receiving of a well appreciated cheque!

My graphics designer Nik, of bookbeaver.co.uk, for his talent in designing the book cover and making my revisions with perfect peace and great customer service.

Peter Branch at peterbphotos.com for his impressive photographic skills in producing my back cover portrait.

David Springer (another graphic designer) who expertly and patiently formatted and laid out the interior of this book. He's a pastor too!

And last, but certainly not least, my daughter Imani, who provoked me to write this book. I often think, if only I could have put the knowledge I now have into my 18 year old body, I would have been a force to be reckoned with. I now do so... but in hers. Hopefully through her and the younger readers of this book, I will have, to some extent, turned around the old adage 'youth is often wasted on the young'.

Introduction

'She's Got That Vibe' is a book for women on how to attract her ideal mate through her authenticity: being true to who she really is and what she truly wants. Too often in this world, we're afraid of being our true selves, for fear of what others may think. This book is not just for women who want to become attraction magnets for men but for those who want to attract the *right* one... by being *themselves*.

Often during dating or relationships, women appear pretentious. This is reflected when she unwittingly sends out vibes that attract responses from men that are contrary to what she really wants. Her exterior actions are at odds with her inner beliefs.

A woman's vibes (which comes from the word vibrations) are the central theme to this book and are explored by examining the top 10 mistakes that turn men off in a dating or relationship situation, so women can understand how men process and respond to a woman's vibes. More specifically, we look at the inner workings of the Law of Attraction (LOA) and how it manages our vibrations to bring about results, both wanted and unwanted.

This uncommon take on the LOA will show women how to own and be their true authentic selves; free from restriction, fear and masks thus allowing them to resonate with life and thus men in an honest and appealing way.

Women, sick and tired of getting unwanted results from their romantic encounters, ask constantly of themselves: why do I always get the wrong guy? Why were things initially great and now sour? Why does dating have to be so frustrating? What am I doing wrong!? This book answers these questions, but more specifically, addresses the types of vibes women are sending out that give rise to these questions in the first place.

I, like many women, have had to address issues on low self-worth, as I *allowed* guys to take me for granted or to take advantage of my supposed naivety. At the time, I played the victim, it was 'poor me'. I didn't know I had to take responsibility for my actions. I didn't think I had the power to change my outcomes.

Over time, I eventually saw these growing pains as opportunities to take responsibility and learn from my mistakes. This was especially apparent when I noticed a cycle of the same lesson being present-ed, just re-packaged differently. When I finally got it, after mastering each lesson, my self-worth would go up a notch and there would be no going back to my former state.

This understanding could not have been realized, had I not personally gone through my fair share of ups and downs, hurts and disappointments. These incidents led me on a quest for further answers as I became a new expanded version of myself and found that the new improved me was better able to manage my love life.

I listened to my girlfriends, repeatedly, tell me their stories of woe and describe in detail what 'he'd done to her' and how 'he'd broken her heart', as if they were pawns, powerless in a game of chess.

I listened to the male point of view as well. Having worked in environmental services for more than ten years-managing a team of 120+ dustmen and being the only female on the team; I –learned a thing or two about the inner workings of a man's mind. They confided in me, openly sharing their stories and views on the behaviours of women. I saw the mistakes we were making, and I grew to understand the 'guy talk'. In fact, I became the 'cool girl', just one of the guys! To this day, I love listening to and working with men.

With this in mind, I conducted a further survey with men in local fitness gyms to gain an insight into how they respond to the vibes women emit and have compiled my findings in a section in this book entitled: The 10 Biggest Mistakes Women Make That Turn Men Off.

Having been a student of self-development for most of my adult life and an avid reader of countless books in this arena, discovering and understanding how The Creator's LOA works has been a game changer for me, as it's proved to be for so many others when used consciously.

The LOA simply states that what you think about, good or bad, you attract in your life. Your thoughts project vibrations and these vibrations attract like-vibrations, drawing to you what you want. We all use the LOA in our everyday lives, but the big secret is, most people don't realize they are doing it.

My intention throughout this book is to provide the tools for women to become aware of the vibes they're giving off – which ones attract and which ones repel. It will also arm them with the ability to effortlessly manifest the attention they desire and how to make unwanted attention disappear.

It was when armed with this arsenal of knowledge that I grew to *know* that as women we are powerful; we are not a victim of our circumstances, and we can take responsibility for who *we allow* in our life. We always attract our perfect match according to who we are 'being' at the time.

It's been wonderful discovering and implementing the information in this book, which I now share with you. My love life has transformed and now takes the shape of mostly happiness; I'm still learning how to live authentically. I am a work in progress, as are we all.

Currently I'm free and single! but only recently so... I was in a relationship where my head said move on, my heart said stay...just a little longer...maybe it'll get better, but deep down I knew. This particular relationship stirred up the 'deep' in me and called up an old wisdom which led to great insight - without it I would not have been able to write this book, the way I have.

There is happiness in being authentic! This book does not *only* serve women who are dating or in relationships, this book is also an advocate for women who are single and are comfortable being so. It's about being 'yourself' and from this place of 'being' all 'right' things are drawn to you. There are gems to be gained in the reading of this book.

If being single makes you happy, at this point in your life, then good for you. You get to choose. If you say yes to romance and all the goodies that go with it, then the content of this book will not prove fruitless and you will have armed yourself ready and able to wield your inner power to attract your ideal relationship! With the information herein you'll see how you can apply what you learn not just to your relationships but to your entire life. You see, from confusion comes clarity and it is under pressure that a diamond is formed.

The woman that has 'that vibe', as depicted in the title of this book is the woman who walks in her shoes of authenticity, she embodies the knowledge of how men respond to her vibes and how she can use the LOA to manage her vibrations to her advantage.

By deliberate intention she chooses her vibe through her thoughts, thus drawing to her what she wants. She knows what she wants and so is an independent thinker. She's not stuck in anyone's opinion of her. She has her own ideals. She does not seek to 'impress'. She remains true to herself. Because of this, she can come across to men as feisty, sassy and edgy but in a playful way. It is these innate qualities that present her to a man as something 'different'. This 'difference' is a conundrum to a man, a mental challenge because she can neither be defined or categorized.

She never ever has to chase a man. Her whole vibe, her whole presence, thoughts, words and posture shouts 'she has no need to!' This powerful woman harnesses and holds her secret inner power, that she is a child of God and seeks no other validation than that which He gives. She is enough. This exudes to observers an indefinable and elusive quality, a certain 'je ne se quoi', literally 'I don't know what', which is charming to many, hence earning her the title 'She's got that Vibe!'

1

Your Vibes Explained: The Power Of Vibrations

Your Vibes – What Is That?

The Meaning Of Vibes

No matter what you say or show to the world, nothing else shouts louder than our vibes. Most of us remain unaware of this and think it's the exterior communication and physical appeal that counts and no-where is this thinking more fixed than in the relationship/dating game.

But the big secret is that deep attraction of the magical kind happens beyond the physical. It happens in that space where personal vibes meet and either resonate magically or inexplicably repel. There are 2 conversations going on, the physical and the non-physical. That's why in a room, two people can be drawn to each other and no words have been spoken.

Many women know that men respond to their vibes which are on par to the signals they send out. However, there is much confusion on this subject as I found while conducting research Here's a snapshot of questions as listed on Yahooanswers.com.

- How does a very easily jealous person manage to have a good relationship without giving off bad vibes?
- Can anyone explain to me what it means to 'give off bad vibes' to people? If I'm doing it how do
  I change it?
- Sexual Vibes.....what are they & how am I giving them off?
- Why do I give off strong vibes?

One response was...

"Gosh...that is kind of hard to explain.....to me it means when I get a weird feeling from a person even when I really don't know them well enough to form an opinion...but I trust my gut."

A definition I found which nicely sums it up is...

Google:
A person's emotional state or the atmosphere of a place as communicated to and felt by others.

What I got from the melee of questions and feed-back was that people knew it was related to 'feelings' and they weren't wrong, but what they lacked was the **science** or the **spiritual** aspect behind the questions and the impact of this knowledge. I knew if they did understand and applied it, their lives would transform.

With the right knowledge, you can change how your life shows up.

So, let's delve in!

The Law Of Attraction

The word vibe comes from the word vibration. Vibes are frequencies, meaning we can feel them. To understand our vibes, we must first look at the Law of Attraction (LOA) and how it responds to and manages the vibes we send out.

Now, some of you have probably heard about the LOA; Psychologists, New Age thinkers and some religious leaders have been talking about the LOA for years, though it gained popularity again when the book 'The Secret' by Rhonda Byrne made waves in 2006, thereafter selling millions of copies around the world. It even made the Oprah Winfrey show!

Wikipedia States:
The law of attraction is the name given to the belief that 'like attracts like' and that by focusing on positive or negative thoughts, one can bring about positive or negative results. This belief is based upon the idea that people and their thoughts are both made from pure energy and the belief that like energy attracts like energy.

Everything is energy. Energy vibrates. You are a vibrational being living in a vibrational Universe. The vibrations that are you and that is everything else is managed by the LOA and it does this by matching 'like vibrations' together.

Everything that's drawn into your life is related to the vibes you emit, because the LOA responds to the vibrations you send out. Like a giant sorting office, it matches vibrations every second; 24/7.

The LOA can bring you spiritual connection, greater health, love, money and virtually anything you want. To understand why the vibes we send out are so important to achieving what we want, we have to take a more in-depth look at this Law.

> *Your thoughts affect your feelings. Your feelings reflect outwards as vibrations. Your vibrations are what attract things to you.*

Have you ever walked into the aftermath of an argument and felt you could cut the air with a knife? Or have you experienced someone walking into a room and felt a dark vibe radiating from them? Or heard terms such as 'he was bristling with anger' or 'she's not on the same wavelength'? What about being attracted to someone, like a moth to a flame or automatically smiling because someone smiles at you? These are experiences of 'feeling' vibrations and it can be negative or positive.

To further understand, let's do this exercise: Think of a happy event. Imagine yourself sending out joyful vibes...how do you feel? Do you think a negative or a positive person would be drawn to you? Now do the same with an unhappy event. Imagine yourself sending out angry vibes. How do you feel? Do you think a negative or a positive person would be drawn to you? Like attracts like.

So What Does 'Like Attracts Like' Really Mean?

It means the Universe will grant you experiences that match and enhance the feelings you are feeling. Your feelings are your vibrations. Responding to the topic and the vibrations you send out around it, the LOA, like a genie in a bottle replies, 'your wish is my command! '

The LOA will provide you proof of what you're feeling on what you're thinking about...

Analogy: The Cave

When you send out your vibes to another, it's not dissimilar to being in a cave and having your words and your vibes bounce right back at you. Like a boomerang effect, *your cave mimics your reality*.

So if you were to physically be in a cave and were to holler out from a place of negativity: 'you're a bitch', 'you're a bitch', 'you're a bitch!', the cave will echo right back at you: 'you're a bitch...you're a bitch...you're a bitch!' and actually amplify your experience, as if to say 'here are your vibrations, right back at you!' Now it's not so much the other person that's a bitch now... is it? You will attract experiences of 'bitchiness' and it is you who now reflects this unattractive quality.

When you bless others and you say 'you're prosperous' and are coming from a genuine place of happiness and well-being for another, the cave bounces right back at you and echoes 'you're prosperous', 'you're prosperous', 'you're prosperous'! Here are these vibrations right back at you: 'you're prosperous!'

You see we ARE all connected and when you bless another, you bless yourself and when you curse another, you curse yourself.

It's all about who you are being in the process. You are a 'BE'ing. So who you 'BE' in the moment is everything.

Life reflects back at you what you're feeling. I'm sure you've been on those movie websites or book sites where the cookies keep track of your likes and displays 'we noticed you like that, so we thought you'd also like these titles'. It works like that.

So How Is This Applicable In A Relationship?

When trying to **attract the type of relationship you want,** can you see why you need to pay attention to how you're feeling about what you're thinking? … as your thoughts and feelings determine your vibrations…which determines your reality.

Now, it's important to note that the Universe responds only to your vibrations. It doesn't respond to your words if they're not synchronised with your feelings. Let me explain. How often have you responded to someone asking, 'How are you today?' and you reply 'fine' when in fact it's the opposite to what you're really feeling. Have you seen in the face of a person about to perform a charity bungee jump pure terror, as they unconvincingly squeal to everyone around them that they're ok?!

Your feelings serve as your emotional guide; they give an indication of where your vibrations are. If you don't feel good, you're sending out vibrations which are not a match with what you really want and if you feel good, your vibrations are a match with what you do want.

CASE

When it comes to tidiness, my teenage daughter is the complete opposite of me. I'm very tidy; untidiness overwhelms me, whereas my daughter just doesn't seem to care. Sometimes I get really angry at her and then I remember that my feelings are my vibrational checkpoint.

Before I would shout, 'this is so untidy! Come and clean up, why do I have to repeat myself? I'm not your maid etc.' I would get so angry... I'm sure some mothers can relate! However, this created more feelings of anger, as what you *focus on expands* and the Universe's unswerving response, every time is 'your wish is my command' and serves up a platter of 'I'll give you more reasons to be angry'. This is more proof of your thoughts. 'Yes! I will give you more of this feeling that you do not want!'

When I use my feelings as my checkpoint and remember that they serve as my guide to let me know whether or not I am on the path to what I want, I can stop and change focus. In the case above, I am clearly sending out negative vibes that pushes away the very thing that I want. I can now change to thoughts that are in harmony to what I really want.

So instead of approaching the situation with anger, I approach it this way, with thoughts of 'wouldn't it be great if this bathroom was kept nice and tidy, it would create such peace in me. I love it when the bath and sink are pristine and smelling of scented products...' Can you see from this standpoint the different feelings it evokes? Now that my emotions are in harmony with what I really want, the LOA will now give me more reasons to feel that way.

Your Emotions Operate On A Sliding Scale

Imagine a ruler: on one end is the positive feeling of **having the thing you want** and on the other end is the negative feeling of the **lack of the thing you want**. In the case above, I was initially coming from a negative vibrational space as I was focused on the 'feeling' of the **lack of what I want**. In other words, my feelings pushed away the very thing I wanted, a tidy bathroom. On the other end, I was coming from a positive vibrational space as I focused on the 'feeling' of having **what I want** thus drawing to me the very thing I wanted: the experience of a tidier bathroom, i.e. more reasons to feel good.

Let's give another example: You have a pile of bills in front of you and you say, 'I wish I had more money'. The LOA reads your vibes of despair and serves you more proof of your feelings. On the flip side, you look at the pile of bills and you imagine them disappearing under a ball of flames and you smile...then you imagine them being replaced by a fat pile of money and it makes you smile even more and you think, 'when I get my money, I'm going to Thailand! I'm going to.......I'm going to.......' fill in the blanks! Can you feel yourself smiling? From this space of vibration, the LOA responds and delivers you more of those feelings.

Another nice way of attracting what you want is to begin by saying, 'it would be so nice if......and then imagine the feelings it evokes. For example at the time of writing, my daughter's friend has ordered a takeout and as she descends the stairs, she sees me and I hear her say to my daughter, 'oh I didn't realise your mum was here, I would have ordered more food'...anyway, my daughter brings me a plate and a drink and I hear my daughter in the kitchen say, 'hey, here's the 2 Cokes.'

And I think aaah, I could really do with a sip of Coke, wouldn't it be nice to have a nice cold sip...and within seconds my daughter is in front of me offering me a sip of Coke from her can....that's the LOA and it can work as fast as that, through the path of least resistance it delivers your requests. Resistance is doubt and is the opposite of 'showing up for' or allowing the result. It's the very thing that cancels out your desire from manifesting.

This feeling/vibrational scale is vital to understand as you are either approaching what you want from an emotion of 'what you want' or an emotion of 'a lack of what you want' and these evoke two contrasting sets of feelings that are key to whether you will receive or not.

You need to be *careful* about what you think about, because you could just as equally be focusing your thoughts on what you *don't want* as opposed to what you *do want*. The more you focus on what you do not want, you hold yourself in a sustained vibration that disallows the very thing that you do want from coming into your reality. In other words you cannot entertain two opposing thoughts at the same time. You cannot think of a 'want' and a 'do not want' at the same time.

'You cannot serve two masters'. *(Matthew 6:24)*

For it is your thoughts that rule you. You are subject to your thoughts. Only thing is, you get to choose.

So understanding and using the LOA as a premise, let's see how we can attract your perfect match by using your powers of vibration.

The 5 Steps To Attracting Your Mate

Ask It~Be~Believe It~Expect It~Allow It

1. **Ask:** First ask for what you want. This part is simple. The Universe already knows what you want, far better than you are consciously aware, as it has kept record of your preferences accrued throughout your lifetime.

2. **Be:** 'like attracts like' so you have to BE the qualities/vibrations that you want to attract. Be the type of person you want to meet. You begin by saying or thinking 'I am _____' and then fill in the blanks with the qualities you wish to attract. You have to *visualise and feel.*

(More on the 'I AM' exercise in workbook, available at www.shesgotthatvibe.com)

a. Think of your ideal partner. Design him. *Make a list of your wants.* Have you seen that movie Weird Science? Write out a description of him. List all the qualities you would like to see in him: is he kind, thoughtful, funny, serious? What does he look like? What does he like to do? Does he like sport, travelling, eating out? Make as detailed a description as you can. Fantasize, as if he's already in your life. Pretend and make believe until you do believe.

b. However, the Universe has a better version of what you could possibly envision so don't be too surprised if you get what you want in a package you did not expect, *the key is to be open* to this and to not be so rigid in your perception as to not recognise him when he appears. Trust in the All-Knowing to deliver what is a match to you.

3. **Believe:** Your belief is what makes it manifest, your belief is what opens the door from the invisible world to your visible world, your reality. A belief is only a thought that you keep thinking, so to change your belief, you must change your thoughts that are a match to what you want.... and you do this by exercising repetitive thoughts until you do believe and then you are on the path to drawing what you want into your experience.

4. **Expect:** 'Show Up'. Expect him to come into your life! Don't doubt. Have faith. If you want a man with certain qualities and you doubt the possibility of attracting him into your reality, your doubt will cancel him away. Your doubt is your resistance to allowing him to come to you. For you to show up for him, you have to be in total alignment with his possibility. He is already there. It is done. Your job is to experience his showing up because you've showed up. Again, it's down to you. It's like sending out an email to the Universe and expecting a response. If there is no expectation, then you will not show up to receive.

5. **Allow**: If, when visualising, you notice any feelings of unease i.e. thoughts that pop up such as 'I don't think I deserve this man I've imagined', then you are experiencing limiting beliefs that are blocking your path to the manifestation of your ideal mate. These thoughts are your doubts and represent your resistance. You must think purely, that means, no doubt!

(More on limiting beliefs in Part 3 of this book)

Can you now see why your vibes are paramount to getting what you want? God's Universe operates on Laws, and when you send out your vibes and your requests, the LOA is activated and sifts through the myriad of vibrations that abound in the Universe bringing like vibrations together. The LOA is at work 24/7 and like the law of gravity, it takes no breaks.

The Art Of Allowing: 'Resistance' Further Explained

Now, it would be remiss of me to not explain the matter of resistance in more depth, as it's vital to your manifestation.

Resistance is when you *do not allow* what you have asked for to come to you. In other words, it's when you do not show up for what you have asked for.

To use an analogy, imagine you've ordered a book from Amazon and you've been told it will be delivered at 10 o'clock the following day. Now, for any number of reasons, you may not show up for the delivery; those reasons could be... the car broke down, you couldn't get out of a meeting, you were in an argument, road rage or simply you forgot...whatever the reason, these obstacles would present a resistance to you not showing up for your delivery.

Doubt:

With the LOA, it is no different. When you present obstacles that disallow you from receiving what you've requested, you get in your own way, by not showing up. Your obstacles are your doubts. The LOA has done its part - it's prepared your order ina world invisible to you. However, when it's time to make it visible and you're not there to receive it, you don't get to experience your order... until such a time, when you do show up. When you do, you are ready to receive. Faith is a state of knowing that in your asking of it, you will receive. Where there is doubt, there lies your resistance to you receiving. The speed of your manifestation is directly related to your level of doubt.

To further explain when your thoughts are the same as your spiritual inner you, which is the best version of you, you are in alignment. You see you have to be on an equal vibration to that of your inner you to receive what has been prepared for you in your asking of it.

Forgiveness:

A harbouring of un-forgiveness is a major obstacle to you not receiving your request. It's like a blockage in a pipeline that restricts and stops your flow and disables you connecting fully with that God part of you.

At its root, the doubts that you have originate from un-forgiveness, either of yourself or another.

A route to you being authentic, i.e. to be one with love – because God is love, is through forgiveness. You see, when you don't forgive it blocks love, it resists love from flowing through you and into different areas of your life. That's why to forgive is so important.

Anything that you can do to release blockages that set you apart from your Creator will lessen your resistance and thus speed up your manifestation of your desire. God wants you in union with Him, not apart.

Forgive yourself - for not thinking that you're enough, because you've told yourself that lie by letting your outward circumstances determine who you are instead of realising it is the other way 'round, it is your inner thoughts that determine your outward world, your reality. When you change your inner thoughts, your outer world bows to you and conforms to who you are now, thus reflecting your desired reality right back at you.

Forgive others - We're all connected and when you have grievance against another, you attract that to yourself. In the bible it puts it like this.

> *Mark 11:22-25 New Living Translation*
> *22 Then Jesus said to the disciples, "Have faith in God. 23 I tell you the truth, you can say to this mountain, 'May you be lifted up and thrown into the sea,' and it will happen. But you must really believe it will happen and have no doubt in your heart. 24 I tell you, you can pray for anything, and if you believe that you've received it, it will be yours. 25 **But when you are praying, first forgive anyone you are holding a grudge against, so that your Father in heaven will forgive your sins, too.**

It's so important that you take time to clean up your vibrations so that your vibrations take full effect and this is done through forgiving. Is there anyone you need to forgive? Your ex-boyfriend, current boyfriend, partner, husband, brother, father or any man that has caused you some perceived harm that's blocking you from allowing your ideal mate to come into your life? Or is it a significant female figure that you've allowed to impact your view on how you see relationships? It doesn't have to be a man....Don't let your un-forgiveness form a barrier to God's Universe *'hearing'* you. You need to start breaking down your walls.

'The hardest prison to escape is in your mind' ...

quote unknown

You Get What You Focus On

Contrasting Experiences

You often don't know 'what you want' unless you experience 'what you don't want'. By this I mean... if you've got a broke boyfriend, you ask for a boyfriend that's got money; if you've got a boyfriend who's a flop in bed (excuse the pun!) you ask for a boyfriend that's great in bed. If he's not that good looking, maybe you ask for a boyfriend that is!   Your wants are acknowledged by the Universe and the LOA taking note of your requests, upgrades the vibrational waves you emit.

So you see, we have a contrast between what we do want and what we do not want. Whenever you become clear on what you want by being aware of what you *do not* want, then your authenticity will take hold. It's hard to be authentic if you don't know what you value and desire.

(Visit www.She'sGotThatVibe.com for workbook of exercises to get clear on what you want)

Claim Your FREE Complementary Workbook
At www.shesgotthatvibe.com/workbook/

Now, bearing this in mind, imagine you're in a restaurant and you're about to order the food you'd like to eat. Would you experience the dishes on the menu that you do want by focusing and complaining about the dishes that you *do not* want? Sounds nonsensical right? So why do it within a relationship?

When you complain about aspects or qualities of a boyfriend that you do not like, guess what you get more of? It takes up space - stopping you from allowing the good to come to you. **What you focus on expands**....so, to get more of what you want, focus on the qualities that you like. Pay attention to the vibrations you're offering up to the Universe by observing your feelings in relation to the results you're getting.

When complaining about your boo you'll always know when you've slipped off track because your emotions will tell you. If you don't feel good, and it's something you've said, then stop and reframe your words in a pleasant way where it is no longer a complaint. For example: your boyfriend doesn't call you enough. Don't criticise, just speak your truth from a place of love, 'It's great speaking with you, I'd love if you would call more often.' Can you see how this is a compliment instead of a complaint? When you are on track and authentic with how you feel, he'll feel that too.

Try speaking more statements that start off with ...'It would be so nice if .....' or, 'I'd feel so much more comfortable if ....' Make the focus on your needs but deliver in such a way that it leaves him and you in a state of well-being. When he feels good, he will do more good. Turn criticism on its head and communicate in a way that leaves you both with a feeling of well-being.

The only way you can stop attracting something that you do not want is to focus your attention to something that you do want...and this can be challenging, particularly if you've trained yourself to a consistent pattern of vibration; this is especially so if you're exiting a relationship or getting over an ex-boyfriend.

However, you can move on in steps by focusing and developing on the thoughts around what you desire. You are not expected to switch off emotionally like a tap. So if you're going through the 'getting over you' process, you may move through a range of feelings, such as hurt and anger to self-pity and powerlessness to numbness to forgiveness to letting go of blame, to hope of better, to asking of something new, to believing, to being, to receiving. Not necessarily in that order, but you get the gist.

We Live In An Inclusive Attraction-Based Universe

By that I mean you cannot shut anything out, you can only change your focus - as we're all energy and we're all connected. For example if I said, **'don't think** of a blue elephant with pink dots', your response is, 'yes! I will not think of this thing that I have been told to not think of' and what do you do? You think of a blue elephant with pink dots! Our inner being in connection with the Universe, a swirling mass of our vibrations, only understands 'Yes'. There is no such thing as 'No'. Only Yes! to our requests.

> *Matthew 7:7 New International Version*
> *'Ask and it will be given to you; seek and you will find; knock and the door will be opened to you...*

The universe only understands your 'feelings' that's how you communicate within. And it says yes every time.

You see when you are confronted with something that you do not want to experience and you shout, 'No!' at it, through your *attention* to it you invite it into your experience and it is now active in your vibration. In this attraction-based Universe, there is no such thing as exclusion. You can only change your experience by what you focus on.

What you resist persists - because you have given your attention to it and what you focus on expands....

It's like baking a cake. You want to bake the perfect chocolate cake. You open the cupboard and there in front of you are all the ingredients required ...*except* there is a bottle of vanilla essence which you do not need...and you look at the vanilla essence and complain.. why is this vanilla essence here? I don't want it in my cake... I don't want it in my cake! ....and so your persistent focus on the vanilla essence doesn't allow for the cake to be made *Yes,* we live in an inclusive Universe and Yes you cannot rid anything from your vibration but you can choose that to which you give your attention.

To clarify, when you look at John, your ex-boyfriend and shout, 'No, I don't want you as a part of my life anymore, go away!' then what you are doing, is calling John into your experience, for there is no such thing as 'No' in an attraction-based Universe. Your very attention to it says, 'Yes, come to me, John that I do not want!' LOA responds to your vibrations, not your no's and don't's.

1. The Universe only says yes; it doesn't understand no's, not's and don't's.

2. It responds powerfully to what you want to BE when you say 'I am...'

3. There is only the positive feeling of the 'thing wanted' or the negative feeling of the 'lack of the thing wanted'

4. Let's refer to the 'thing wanted' as the topic

5. The Universe responds to the topic and your feelings around it

6. Your words do not always match what you feel/ vibrations

7. Make sure your words match what you want

8. When you feel appreciation for what you want it sends out a vibration of well-being which you attract back

9. When you feel despair from a lack of a thing wanted, it pushes it away

10. The Universe doesn't recognise a vibrational difference between your reality and what is imagined

Below, I will share two stories which we will later scrutinise from a vibrational perspective. These are true stories, however for privacy, names have been changed.

STORY NO.1:

The 'When Sally Met Harry' Story – From Sally's Perspective

Once upon a time, a woman named Sally met Harry. Harry said to her that he'd always liked her and he cited some places that he'd spotted her over a span of 10 years Sally was very surprised as, to her mind, it was her first time of meeting him. However, Sally was attracted to him, a courtship began and they began to date lightly for 9 months until they both decided to exclusively date each other.

Unbeknown to Harry, one of the reasons Sally had taken a while to get closer to him was due to emotional feelings carried for a previous boyfriend and so she had been unsure if it would be the right thing to draw closer to him. Despite this, she opened her heart to Harry and they did grow closer.

Harry also had his emotional baggage, he was separated, or so he said, but she believed him. She'd never been to his place where he said he resided with his brother and he'd never taken her there because he said his brother was a Christian and would not approve, oh! and neither his mother.. Harry was 47 years old. He was also married with kids and would be at the family home every weekend, at least, that's what he said. Of course he had to see the kids and besides he was building an extension that he'd made a commitment to do... for the kids. Sally didn't know these addresses, just the general area...well, that's what he said.

Anyway, they continued in this vein of seeing each other, once a happy night, every Friday night and it was always a happy night. As months went by and Sally resolved her emotional baggage, she began to feel emotionally closer to Harry and so her desires and wants changed and she wanted more.

One summer's day, 14 months from their initial date, Sally expressed her wanting for more. She told him she would like for him to get a place so she could go visit him and perhaps sleep over occasionally and then that way the relationship would feel more like '50/50'. After a long chat, Harry said to give him till November (another 6 months) as he had some commitments. November came and went; there was no sign of the apartment that Harry said he would get. She confronted him. He said he had moved the deadline because he had other commitments to fulfil in relation to his mother and so right now to get a flat would be a misappropriation of funds. Sally was very disappointed.

She felt as if she came last and her hurt and disappointment grew... 'how could he change his mind like that without speaking to her on the matter? Did he realise how important this had been to her? Had he had any intention at all of getting an apartment? Was it just a strategy to draw as many 'happy nights' out of her as he could?' She felt like a fool! He clearly didn't prioritise the relationship as she did and so the thoughts kept coming. She felt very sad. 'How could I have been so stupid...?' the thoughts went on and on....her self-worth dipped and as she blamed him for wasting her time, Harry withdrew.

Maybe he felt guilty. Who knows...anyway he distanced himself as she made him feel bad, by her distrust, her anger, her criticism and so eventually after an exchange of painful remarks and a fanfare of her tears they parted That was the end of 'happy nights' on a Friday.

THE END

Now we could be indignantly judgemental and state, he clearly strung her along, she was very naïve, or so foolish..he provided no evidence of his circumstances etc. etc. etc. However wherein does her power lie?... As mentioned, let's take a look at this story from the perspective of the LOA and how the power of her vibrations played its part.

When Sally met Harry, they were vibrationally matched. Harry was happy. Sally was happy; you see they both needed an element of space from each other for their own private reasons. She attracted someone of a like mind-set and so did he. Because their vibrations were aligned and the LOA must provide proof of their sustained vibrations, the Universe put them together.

At some point Sally's wants changed, she wanted more. Harry's wants remained the same. They became a vibrational mismatch to each other. When Sally zigged, Harry zagged.

Because Sally's wants had changed she wanted her wants to be met by Harry. When Harry did not meet her wants she zigged and zigged and zigged. Was it unfair of Sally to now expect Harry to meet her wants and her expectations? Was it unfair of Sally to now ask Harry to 'be' the person of change to make her happy?

To be responsible for her happiness? Harry was consistent. Harry had remained the same.

Sally was then introduced to the LOA. Sally realised Harry was just selfishly being true to himself and that likewise she needed to be true to herself and that through her thoughts, her vibrations, she could consciously choose and attract her perfect match.

She realised she had been caught up in the details of the relationship, and was in a sustained vibe of complaint as what she focused on expanded and it was this that was holding her back from what she really wanted. From now on she resolved to consciously try to focus on her wants and not her 'not wants'. It was focusing on her 'not wants' through a mode of complaint that pushed what she wanted away.

Just digest those thoughts for a moment. Sally was using the details of this relationship to hold her back, in a pattern of not moving on. Harry was provoking her into growth of wanting more, but Harry did not want this and so did not meet her expectations because he was selfishly focused on his own desires and what made him happy.

"We live in a world of contrasts and if it were not for the contrasts, you couldn't ask for the improvement, but the very contrast that is responsible for the improvement, you use as your excuse not to go... with the improvement"

Abraham Hicks

"When one door of happiness closes, another opens; but often we look so long at the closed door that we do not see the one which has been opened for us."

Helen Keller

We're all selfishly focused, that's why in a group picture, the first person you seek out will be yourself; that is our true and instinctive nature and so you can see it's not a bad thing as the world would have you think. It's only so when it's at the detriment of others. In the context of which I am speaking, selfish equates to self-care.

A man is not supposed to do everything to make you feel better or happy; that's not his job. In fact it's impossible. His responsibility is to be true to himself as it is yours to be true to you. It's your responsibility to make yourself happy through the power of the thoughts/vibes that only you can choose. You both enhance each other's happiness.

In their inauthenticity, a lot of women are unhappy and anxious in their relationships; it's about owning who you are and being responsible for yourself.

You see, what a lot of people do is they choose their mate, expecting to seek from them qualities that they themselves lack. For example, they expect respect, when they do not have respect for themselves. They expect generosity when they themselves are not generous. Do not seek your mate to complement your lack, instead come to him as a 'whole' person; by this I mean 'be' the quality you seek, so you can attract it from your partner. Remember, 'like attracts like'.

STORY NO.2 - The Shanice Story

Telephone Conversation 1:

Best Friend. 'Hey Shanice, would you like to come Salsa tonight?'

Shanice: 'I best not, John hates it when I dance Salsa, he's thinks it's too flirty.'

Best Friend: 'But you love Salsa!'

Shanice: 'I know, she says longingly, but he'll only get angry.'

Telephone conversation 2:

Friend: 'Hey Shans, wanna meet up this Sunday?'

Shanice: 'Oh I can't, John is coming over. (Big sighs)... I do get tired sometimes, I feel like my weekend is not mine anymore and he needs so much pampering: he wants a massage, I have to cook, and you know I don't really cook that much, and as soon as I've finished one thing, he wants me to do something else, I just don't get a chance to really relax!'

Friend: 'But Shans, you work all week, really hard, what about your needs? Don't you feel you're going to resent this at some point?'

Shanice: 'I know... but he does so much for me, he treats me to so much, he buys me clothes, little gifts, he does give back.'

Friend: 'But Shans, who are you trying to convince? You're gonna need to talk to him about it, maybe he doesn't even realise he's being too demanding; you're not being true to who you really are.'

STORY NO.3 - The Shanice Story

As Jennifer looked around the table she noticed that Shanice and John sat stone-faced as they looked at the comedy act on stage. They were all sat in a show/dance event and Shanice had whispered to Jennifer earlier on that John was not happy with how disorganised everything was....and it showed.

After the show and as the dance commenced, music on, people rocking, Jenny looked to pull Shanice to the dance floor but she declined. She said, 'You know if it was just you and I, I'd be on the dance floor enjoying myself, but I know if I do, he'll just get upset and feel that I'm disrespecting him, so I better not, in fact I think I'm gonna go home,' and so they both left.

Moral of stories: When in a relationship, it's always good to ask yourself the questions: 'What is this relationship doing for me? Is it what I want?' You see, if you're not yourself then you're not free to be the girlfriend, partner, wife you want to be. You're being what he wants you to be. Don't betray your authenticity by selling yourself short so that you can live up to someone else's opinions, expectations, and standards. You've got to be you. Go on, try it, just try being you and you'll see how, when you live with integrity, people take you more seriously.

- Stop focussing on the other person's wants, thus disallowing your own wants.
- Do not blame your boo for you not getting what you want.
- You should never give up 'who you are' as a reward for another's kindness.
- Learn to communicate your wants in a way that is not a criticism

Thoughts Of A 'She's Got That Vibe' Woman

1. I do not depend on another to meet all my needs.

2. They will inevitably let me down every time because it's not their job.

3. It's not their job to make me whole. That's my job.

4. I find my preferences from my contrasting experiences and I 'be' the change I want, so it becomes active in my vibration and so I will attract it.

5. I am disciplined in my thoughts to attract what I want.

6. I think about it, visualise it and fantasise with it.

7. I don't pick a person and then ask them to match my preferences, that would be unfair

8. I don't ask the person to become what I want so I can have what I want.

9. It's not their responsibility to be everything that I want.

10. That's my responsibility...

11. I tell my girlfriends, stop looking at that person who caused you to want more and then blaming them for your emotional dis-harmony.

12. If you think a thought that is different to what you want, change it; don't train your thoughts into a pattern that hold you apart from what you want.

13. Develop your own deliberate pattern of thoughts.

14. Stop focussing on the other person's wants, thus disallowing your own wants.

15. Stop blaming the other person for you not getting what you want.

16. Be the only player to attracting what you want.

17. Stop asking others to be major players in what you want.

18. Become a vibrational match to what you want.

19. What comes to you is what's active in your vibration.

20. In other words, cut him some slack!

21. Often you can get what you want from what you got.

22. Actively change your thoughts around what you want and create a whole new vibration.

Traits Of An Authentic Woman...

When God made you, He created you as a one-off, a masterpiece; He stamped His seal of approval on you and said you are enough. When you walk in this knowledge, you will never seek from another validation as to who you are; the only validation that you need is that from your Creator.

When you walk in *inauthenticity* you dishonour your Creator: it's like you're saying, you did not create me 'enough'. When you walk in *inauthenticity* you are buying into a false illusion, a lie, of who you really are. As you walk about in a distorted version of who you are, you feel a void, something is not right, something is missing and so you seek the validation of others to make you feel whole. When you walk in *inauthenticity* you are walking in an illusion, you are walking in fear, to quote the acronym: false evidence appearing real.

When you walk in your authenticity, you know you are a child of the Most High, thus you hold your head high and nothing fazes you. All things are subject to you, yes, even the LOA. Others will look at you and see you as a shining light, almost as a beacon calling them to do the same. There is nothing more powerful than a woman who walks in her birth-right.

2

How Men Respond To Negative Vibrations:

The Top 10 Biggest Mistakes Women Make That Turn Men Off!

The Top 10 Biggest Mistakes Women Make That Turn Men Off

You now have an understanding of how the LOA works and what it takes to get your vibrations in check; that it's your inner dialogue that a man reads and decides whether you're a keeper or the grim reaper. You can apply this knowledge right now to attract your ideal mate and stop inadvertently turning off good men and turning on the wrong men!

The following top 10 mistakes that turn men off are a perfect reflection of how you may be doing just this. These mistakes are not set in stone but seem to be a general consensus among men. They are a picture of the unwanted outcomes. Practical advice is provided to avoid these mistakes, whilst on your way to your ideal relationship.

So with this in mind let's take a look at how life is, perhaps, currently showing up for you by looking at these mistakes which allow us to observe the way men respond to a woman's negative vibrations; that way, you have a personal insight and can make any changes required. No more wasted opportunities!

Whilst reading these mistakes, keep a sense of humour. If you notice instances of your inauthenticity, just acknowledge it without judging yourself. Don't beat yourself up about it, laugh and move on; you see when a woman is unaware of her mistakes, it is in her self-awareness that the mistakes disappear. Observing our mistakes is like holding up a mirror, motivating us to be the person we really want to be.

The mistakes made highlight your disconnect from your authenticity and it is this that a man picks up on. As mentioned, there are really always two conversations going on: that which is physical and that which is non-physical: your thoughts, your inner dialogue. When the two are at a mismatch - your *inauthenticity* comes through as opposed to your authenticity....and makes the man run for cover.

Your authenticity requires you to accept your strengths and your weaknesses and in your transparency and your vulnerability, that's when you really shine through! When you're being genuine and real it allows you to connect deeply with others... and in turn you will attract this from them too.

So...let's hold hands and take a peek through the looking glass.

Mistake #1:
Pursuing Men

A man cannot pursue a woman that is pursuing him. Think about that for a moment. The pursuer cannot be the pursued. So women, if you want to be the pursued, stop chasing him.

Women that do this are violating a psychological and biological natural law and delivered straight from the mouths of those in the know, when you do this you are killing his attraction for you.

Basic biology dictates that it's the sperm that chases the egg...not the other way round! When the sperm enters the space of the egg, it is survival of the fittest. It is the most competent sperm that wins the prize... and you are a prize, aren't you?

Men are competitive beings. Ego driven, they like racing cars, football, basketball and hunting! Back in the day, fox hunting was a big thing, the enjoyment being

Claim Your FREE Complementary Workbook
At www.shesgotthatvibe.com/workbook/

in the thrill of the chase! When the fox is finally caught it's regarded as a prize, a trophy. Tell me...would it be the same if that same fox was just handed over on a plate?... nobody values a freebie.

Another example, when you were a kid what did you value more, the pocket money given or the pocket money earned? What is of more value, the diamond or the lump of coal? Anything hard to get, that you have to invest time and effort to acquire, you will value. This is human nature.

So knowing this, why do some women present themselves to men on a plate?

Because she thinks she's not worthy? What do her vibes say? Are they saying, 'I feel inadequate', therefore creating a premise for the LOA to bring her more reasons to feel so?

If you're making most of the phone-calls, sending most of the texts, initiating most of the dates, giving up time with your girlfriends and your hobbies and interests, doing most of the 'driving out' to see him, being available at his convenience at short notice; asking questions like 'where do you see this relationship going?' or 'can you see us having a future?' STOP! and understand this: you are the pursuer and you are chasing him ...away!

When a woman makes a man the centre of her world and loses herself, she is chasing a fantasy, as it's based on false expectations which form a false reality. When you compromise your own needs to satisfy those of a man, you have put your needs on the backburner, effectively placing yourself last.

I believe that every woman who has ever loved, to some degree, myself included has succumbed to this. Thinking back to those moments make me cringe ....err... swiftly moving on ....but hey at the time, to be light on myself , I didn't know any better and I've learnt! ..and so will you if you happen to identify yourself on this one.

The thing to do is, check your vibrations. Observe how you are feeling - if you're feeling any negative emotions, you're not being true to who you really are and what you really want.

Relax and hold your space, just like the egg in the ovary and allow him to come to you. Position yourself 'figuratively' in front of him and not 'behind him' so he can chase you and you do this by simply dropping all of the behaviours mentioned above. It's that simple. Just be still and feel 'complete', feel 'whole'. Your actions will naturally follow suit. When you feel this way, your vibes will read to a man: 'I don't need you to make me feel happy'. This air of confidence will draw the man in. Please note when a man 'chases' you, he is in effect taking the lead in the relationship...or so he thinks...

A male friend of mine shared this story with me about his ex-girlfriend. He said his girl would turn up at his place occasionally and often it would be when he needed his own space. He would deliberately pick a fight with her to get her to leave and when she would, he would feel guilty. However, more often than not she would call to apologise for the argument that he knew he had started! This type of desperation to keep him, made him lose respect and needless to say they parted. It's a turn-off for men when they see you playing a part they should.

Just being yourself and being observed by another for doing this is so attractive and magnetizing. You don't have to over-think, please others and pretend to be something you are not. Just be you.

Don't crowd the 'space' a man needs to step into to chase you. When you disallow a man from doing this, you are actually stripping away at his manliness and it's this that will push him away as you are not allowing him to be the man that he is. Stop trying to control the relationship. A man shows his love by 'giving' and if you're doing his job for him by over-compensating, how can he step into his role and 'be' who he is?

Sometimes a woman feels the need to reciprocate when a man pleases her. You don't. All you need is to learn to be still and receive. Even God said it, *'Be still and know that I am God." Ps 46v10.* The only reciprocation a man needs is to feel good in your presence and for you to feel good in his, that way you're letting him feel that he's fulfilling his role as a man. That's why a secure woman is so attractive to him. She allows him to be who he is, the hunter, the pursuer, the man.

A man also has to feel that you are not dependent on him for your happiness....this quality alone is unique to him and will make him feel protective towards you, like he doesn't want any other man around his special catch!

One final trick ladies, to help you stay in control of your 'pursuing' – and this works for me.

Create good 'tension' in your relationship. In other words never let a man feel like he has a 100% hold over you...and think about it, he couldn't possibly as he doesn't own your mind. Imagine you are standing, facing your partner and you have a great big elastic band around your bodies holding you together, but there's still a gap between your bodies, enough to cause a slight tension in the band.

As you step backwards against the band, he is pulled forwards to you. When you step forwards, he backs off from you... to maintain the tension. See the analogy? ...and so this is how the game of 'pursuing' goes. The trick is to never let the elastic band get too slack, i.e. no tension, which happens when you're too close to each other - create that tension by keeping yourselves a little apart.

It's 'in the tension' that exciting things happen! thus you'll never get bored of one another. Just make sure you're the one stepping backwards! You're the one that's leading! Next time you find yourself doing too much, ask yourself, am I stepping forward or stepping back? In the words of Goldilocks And The Three Bears...you can feel when the 'tension' is just right.

I was inspired to this 'rubber band' analogy over 20 years ago by the infamous Men Are From Mars and Women Are From Venus author, Dr John Gray.

So in summary, be yourself, and allow him to feel wonderful and uplifted in your presence, to be able to be the man for you. It is this that will cause him to come back again and again.

Mistake #2:
Sleeping On A First Date

If you sleep with a man on your first date, how do you feel about it? Is this action in alignment with what you want? Do you feel good and emotionally stable? Do you not give a damn about what the guy thinks as you're only looking for a bit of fun? Yes? Then hey, if it genuinely makes you feel good, who am I to stop you?

However, more often than not, if you're sleeping with a guy on a first date because you *feel* compelled to do so, it's likely because of low self-worth. If you're not aligned to who you really are and what you really want, then don't! It's all about who you are 'being' when you do this. So bearing this in mind if your goal is for a *long term relationship*, follow this advice: KEEP THE COOKIE JAR CLOSED!

If you were to sleep with him straightaway, he may think that he's not that special and that any guy can get to you as easily as he did. What vibes are you giving off?

I recently watched the TV drama series, 'The Tudors' and it was interesting to hear the advice given to Jane Seymour by her father, 'If you want him to grow to love you, then you cannot be an easy conquest!' He was of course referring to her relationship with Henry VIII. She heeded his advice; Jane later became his Queen!

As previously mentioned, men are primarily hunters. No self-respecting, quality man wants a woman who cannot honour him with the thrill of the chase. Men love to chase women. If you give up the cookies too soon, game over.

So, if you're looking for Mr Right, you don't want him to categorize you as sex only, i.e. short term. You want a quality guy to view you as having enough worth for a long term relationship.

That's why you must think and act in a quality way. If you send out the vibe that you're a quality woman, that's what you'll attract back, a quality man. The ones that aren't quality will run away, because, being at a different vibrational level, they won't want to wait, they won't want to pay the right price for you and so those guys will naturally be disqualified.

That's why it's important that you don't sleep with a guy who is not yet emotionally connected to you, he'll just see it as cheap sex, and I say 'cheap' because he didn't have to work hard for it. You set the price and the standards; it's all down to you. You're in control. So set your vibes high, in line with what you're truly worth and you'll know the price because you'll feel it when anyone approaches you with anything less than what you're worth.

Often-times you can feel when a guy is, or is attempting to devalue you, as if to test you, he pushes at your boundaries to see whether you will give way to something less ...don't succumb. Sometimes, it can be difficult to articulate why you feel a particular way, when this has happened to me I just feel it...trust your gut and withdraw if you need to, to get to grips with the reason for your feeling. When in doubt, don't.

Now when out dating, don't bring condoms with you on a first date. If you think you may be tempted and that you may succumb to his charm, follow the advice of the girl in the movie, 'Think Like A Man' and wear distasteful underwear that you wouldn't be caught dead in! In the movie, she followed the '90 day rule, i.e. no sex for 90 days! Practice withholding yourself and you'll see your true power.

Also, when he drops you home, DON'T invite him in for coffee, as he'll only be looking to dip his biscuit and I'm not talking about into his coffee!

Let him wait, if he has the intellectual ability to wait for delayed sexual gratification then he's a keeper, because by then you should be emotionally connected and thus able to sustain a healthier long term relationship.

Mistake #3:
Dress Code To Run From

Dressing inappropriately, particularly for your age, is quite high on this list for good reason.

Men are attracted to shiny things. So for you to stay shiny this means dressing to suit your figure, accessorizing, and looking good!

The way you dress can either give off a negative or a positive vibe. Your dress code is a reflection of the lens through which you see yourself, i.e. your self-respect, your self-confidence, and it is a physical summation of the vibes you are projecting to those who see you.

When you wear clothes that are too revealing a man can make the assumption, rightly or wrongly, that you haven't got much going for you, other than your body. Don't give him the opportunity to view you as a dumb blonde; as whether you're a brunette, redhead or otherwise, you'll be put in the same category.

An overly sexy outer appearance will send out strong sexual vibes and it may get heads turning and will get you a date, but will it be for the right reasons? Will it match your goal in getting the man of your dreams? Your looks may attract a man, but they will not hold him.

When I was in my early 20's, when out one night at a club, an older friend of mine commented on my dress code. At the time, I thought she was being an old 'fuddy duddy'. As I matured I understood what she meant, my overly sexy attire over my naturally sexy and curvaceous figure were driving the guys wild and attracting the wrong type of guys and repelling the right kind of guys which of course is what I really wanted. At the time, it was my way of looking for love.

When a woman shows less skin, it works on a man's imagination, makes his mind wander and want to see more. It seduces him...

That's why guys love librarian type looking girls. You've seen the type. Shirts done up to the collar, long length skirt with a small discreet slit up the side - as she bends over to collect her books, you see a whisper of her hair against the naked nape of her neck. I'm not saying you should dress like a nun or be overly conservative but you get the picture, leave something to the imagination.

When a woman shows a little but not all, it alludes to a man that he has to work for it and men love mental challenges. Her privileged parts are for the chosen few. Remember whatever is worked hard for in life is valued and in this case, it's no different!

You need to connect to his emotional side as opposed to his sexual side. A woman's tongue-drooling attire can bring out the dog in a man and cause him to be so consumed with lust that he doesn't even hear the words that come out of her mouth, so women: Stop DISTRACTING him! Don't you know that a man can be physically attracted to a woman and yet NOT want a relationship with her? Some women tend to confuse the two.

So...

- Don't wear your thongs up to your hips exposing the strings above the waist line of your skirt or trousers.

- Don't wear transparent clothes that show off your underwear.

- Don't wear miniskirts that could double up as a belt!

- Don't show legs and cleavage together, keep it to either/or.

- Don't wear a bad weave – yes, I said it! That's part of your dress code too – 'cause you're wearing it!

- Don't wear chipped nail polish and unfiled fingernails, keep it neat.

(Focus on the 'do's and not the don'ts', you get the picture!)

He will be attracted to a wo an who makes it a priority to keep up her appearance. I always say, if you want to attract an attractive man then you should be that way too. Keep it sassy but classy!

Aside from that, work on your inner beauty. Men love beauty and can become infatuated but if the inner beauty is not there, your outer beauty will not hold him and he'll put you in the 'fun' category as opposed to the 'keeper'. For a committed, long-lasting relationship, men look for substance, so work on your inner vibe.

Believe in your heart that you're worthy, that you're enough and that you are whole. So when you do meet the man of your dreams you'll be so 'whole' that you will not feel the need to overcompensate by dressing overly sexy. You're sexy enough and attractive enough and he'll see that.

So get your dress code right, as you don't get a second chance to make a first impression.

Mistake #4:
The X-Boyfriend/Other Women

You can't start the next chapter of your life if you keep re-reading the last one. You need to clean up your act at a vibrational level.

Most people do not end and begin their new relationship on good vibes. Instead they move on and carry the old vibes with them and get a new relationship just like the old one and then another and then another. I know of someone who kept on attracting married men. She would say, 'why do I keep attracting married men?'

My response is, take time to clean up your vibes and get into alignment with what you want and then allow the LOA to carve out wonderful relationships for you. Like most people you just observe the unwanted and then complain about it, without first looking in the mirror.

I remember a time I was seeing this guy, we were having a seemingly normal conversation when he turned round and suddenly said, 'Babe, why do you do that?' I responded, hesitantly and quite oblivious to what he was referring to, 'do what?' He said, 'Whenever I say something to you, you always seem to question it, as if not to take me at face value...' As he began to further explain, in a flash, like a revelation, I realised what he meant. I was carrying baggage from a previous relationship.

You see, my ex and father of my child had a habit of asking me seemingly innocent questions like, 'so... where did you go today?' He was an abusive man and I would search my mind frantically for what inappropriate action or man I had been speaking to...where had I been...? I knew he was really addressing another issue. In that moment I realised I had adopted the same approach with my lovely new boyfriend. When he would say something, instead of accepting his words, I would translate his words in my mind to 'so what does he really mean?' In that moment, I woke up and in my awareness, didn't do it again. At least, I hope not! I cleaned up that vibration. I will forever be grateful to him for showing me my unconscious inner dialogue.

So, I advise my girls, when on dates avoid talking about the ex-boyfriend(s) at least in depth as this can give the perception that they're not yet over a past relationship, also, depending on what's said, they can come across as needy and unattractive.

How so? When you say awful complaining things about your ex, this can backfire on you and have your potential partner viewing you in a negative light, that it is you who has the emotional baggage which he will be the brunt of, should he decide to get involved with you.

On the vibrational scale with **what you want** at one end and the **absence of what you want** at the other end; when you speak of what you want from a happy feeling place, you attract experiences to enhance that and you get more of it. However when you speak from a place of not having what you want and so are therefore feeling negative and in a complaining mode, the Universe responds to your feelings, giving you more of that.

And so your date will play out this way... he will use the vibes you are giving off and what you say to judge your character based on the way you interacted with your past partners. For example, if you mentioned that your past partner treated you wonderfully, he's more likely to think, hmmm, she must be a great catch and respond to you with positive vibes. If, on the other hand you complain about him, he may look at you as you're the one with the problems. Don't give him leeway to do so. Manage your vibes.

Additionally, a guy will determine how best to treat you, or at what level to treat you, based on how you speak about your past relationships. For example if what you divulge suggests to him that you do not place a high value on yourself, then why should he?

Moral of the story, the less information you give the better. Men like mystery. Don't be an open book. Get your vibes in order.

Keep your 'story' about the ex-boyfriend to a minimum. For example, if he asks why you parted, you can say 'we parted amicably' or 'we grew apart' or 'he's a great guy and we parted on good terms'. There is a difference between honesty and disclosure.

If you have no desire to listen to stories about his ex-partners, then take charge and politely change the conversation. Simples!

Mistake #5:
Not Having A Voice

Men are attracted to women who can speak their mind, so begin your dating relationship with a voice.

A man wants a woman who has a mind of her own. In other words she has an opinion. She is not afraid to say, 'let's agree to disagree'. She knows her likes and dislikes. She knows what she will tolerate from what she won't tolerate. She has boundaries. Simply, the way you assert yourself lets him know whether you have self-confidence. When you don't assert yourself verbally a man will assume his power over you.

When you're at a restaurant and presented with the menu, choose what you want confidently. Initiate topics of conversation, knowing that your opinion matters and that your opinion is just as valid as his. If he asks, 'what do you like to do?' answer enthusiastically. For example, if you like to read, let him know your preferred genre of books and let this be a topic of conversation.

Visit the gym a few times a week? Describe your preferred work-outs, whether it's Pilates, Yoga or just simply discuss your health interests. Going to the movies? Have a choice of film you'd like to see, don't always let him choose. Again, have a voice, have an opinion.

Another thing that some women have a hard time with are compliments. Accept compliments gracefully. If he comments on your outfit or a pretty dress you're wearing, don't reject the compliment by responding, 'oh, this old thing!' Simply say in a grateful and graceful voice, 'thank you'.

Don't be afraid to express yourself. Be enthusiastic, passionate and show him that you have a zest for life!

You see, when you appear confident, it lets him know that you're not to be easily trifled with and that you can stand up for yourself. So if he behaves badly or tries to take advantage, you can put him in his place. Men find this sexy and again lends to his appetite for a mental challenge.

Some women disservice themselves when they speak negatively. Not just when speaking badly of ex-partners but when speaking negatively of other women.

Now the latter is a BIG one, it's a HUGE turnoff for men. When you make derogatory comments about another woman including name calling such as bitch or slut and the other woman is clearly attractive and desirable, your date will see through you, as coming from a place of insecurity, i.e. demeaning another in order to elevate yourself.

Your fear that he may find the woman more desirable than you is plain to see and he will perceive you as one that will always need validation, as did the witch in the Snow White story, 'Mirror, mirror on the wall, who is the fairest of us all?'.

Not only will it highlight your insecurity and lack of self-confidence but most of all that you are not NICE. Based on this, you may never see your date again.

A woman that knows her self-worth doesn't compare herself against another but is strong, dignified and happy in whom she is.

Ever been in a situation when you're out with your date and an attractive girl enters the room and he turns to look at her? What did you do? Hopefully, you remained calm, poised and collected, as if you didn't even notice. Maybe you even pointed her out and complimented her appearance in some way. Well done to those ladies, you just got a high five!

When you point out others as unattractive, on a vibrational level you send out that you are unattractive and in that moment to the observer, you become exactly that.

There will always be women that are prettier and smarter than you and women that are less so, but there will only be one *you*. You are unique. Be comfortable in your own skin and who you are and hold yourself with self-worth. There's nothing more attractive to a man than a woman with dignity.

When you act like a prize, that's exactly how he'll see you. A quality man wants a strong woman, one who holds herself well and whom he considers his match. Always aim to be positive and happy. Happy is sexy.

Practice your vibrations in relation to what you want your personality to be. The relationship you have with your inner self is the *most important* and comes first before any relationship with another. Be confident and seek ways to raise your self-worth to be secure in who you are and what you are seeking to become.

Your happiness is not dependent on another's behaviour or reaction. When you look at someone and they cause you to feel awful, that is lack of self-worth and there are a variety of ways on how you can reme-dy this which are outside the scope of this book. Just know that when you hold yourself apart from your inner being, which is evident in your bad feeling, this puts you out of alignment to what you are aspiring.

When you criticise and complain, the Universe will reflect back at you more reasons to criticise and com-plain, as what you focus on expands. Care more about your response to you than his response to you and do not seek his approval or validation, you don't need it. You are good enough. Your well-being is the basis of everything good that comes to you. Try this and see how people around you magically change in their atti-tude towards you.

Mistake #6:
Wanting To Be Right

There is nothing worse than a confrontational, argumentative woman that always needs to be right. I'm not saying that a woman shouldn't have an opinion or disagree, I'm saying there's no need to force a point if what we're seeking is a harmonious relationship.

In support of women's liberation and feminism, some women go overboard when it comes to expressing their opinion. Yes, when at work we often cloak ourselves in our masculine energy as we lead, direct, take control and make decisions. That's all well and good sisters, but when you're with a man, take off that masculine vibe and step into your feminine vibe.

Your feminine vibe is power. On the surface, it may seem as if you forcing a point is a sign of strength, but it isn't. Instead, use your femininity to reduce conflict. Look at the way the lady in the movie Hulk uses her gentleness and persuasiveness to manage the massive, testosterone, sweetie and how her 'energy' calms him down.

When you're forceful with a man, it brings out his urge to compete as he sees it as an attempt to emasculate him. Feminism is not about force. It's about acknowledging and embracing your feminine strength to your advantage, not being and acting like a man.

Women are innately compelling and it's unnatural in our make-up to compete with a man or our mate. We're lovers not fighters, therein lies our power. Whenever you exercise your soft side, it appeals to his need to protect. Let your man be a man and have his token of power.

When a woman seeks to have the last say or 'one up' on the man, challenging every little thing that he says, it's a big turn off. If you do have disagreements that you need to resolve, do it privately and not in public, and especially not in the company of mutual friends as you'll diminish his significance.

It's important that a man feels significant and he does this via his social status and this is all wrapped up in who he is. This is defined by what he does and who he is perceived to be. People around him can either make him feel significant or disrespected. Which role do you choose?

Men, particularly those with high-powered jobs and stressful careers, often go head to head with co-workers and customers. The last thing they need is more stress from the woman in their life. Be caring, playful and sexy.

Naturally, it's nice to be around someone who makes you feel good and it makes him feel good that he's making you happy. Remember, like you, men have a choice with whom they spend their time with and no-one wants to be around someone who puts pressure on them by making them feel as if they're responsible for their happiness or lack of.

A man has a deep-seated need to feel that he's right. That he's the chief. This works hand in hand with his ego and his need for that feeling of control. Power is to a man, as romance is to a woman. This feeling is a big turn on for a man. So why not give him his play? Ladies we know we're the ones with the leverage.

I remember an incident in church, which to me encapsulated a woman's understanding of leverage. After a particularly powerful sermon on the man's lead role in the family, I heard an old girl whisper conspiratorially, as she leaned over to her neighbour, 'My husband may be the head of the house, but remember the head can't turn without the neck!' ....and we know who the neck is don't we? So just relax, use your natural feminine charm in a SMART way to get what you want.

If your goal is to have a harmonious happy relationship, it's not about scoring points as to who's wrong or right and if it takes you being demure and soft to give him his sense of control, so be it. It doesn't mean you're weak, it just means you understand the power of your femininity. This is leverage.

When you're in alignment with your inner being you don't 'need' to be right. You're enough all on your own. You are whole. Those who see themselves as whole, make no demands. You are not stuck or dependent on the views of another, in other words you do not seek or need another's validation. You care neither if they agree or disagree, as you are secure in yourself.

When you earnestly seek another's approval in your need to be right, you are in effect handing over your power to that person and you are saying, 'your view is more important than mine and I need you to make me feel *right*', in other words, ' complete'.

So, let go of the need to be right and direct your thoughts to being 'whole'. When you are whole you seek nothing outside of yourself to make you complete, for you already are. The need to be right is in opposition to your feminine power and to the loving inner being that you truly are.

Mistake #7:

Too Much Too Soon

When a guy invites you out on a date, don't be 'too much of anything!' Don't be too touchy-feely on your first couple of dates as he's unfamiliar and you've not yet established an emotional connection. Keep your hands to yourself and remember you're trying to work out if he meets your criteria, if there are common interests and simply if you like him.

So, no inappropriate moves; even if you fancy him like crazy, even if you're overwhelmed by chemical reactions and you've simply not had you some in a long... long...very long time...resist the urge!

If you're at your first dinner date, don't touch his fingers over candlelight, remain composed. If you're out at the movies, don't slip your hands between his legs and 'accidentally' brush against his meat and two veg, exclaiming as if shocked, 'Ooh! What a big Burrito you have'; he'll assume you're open to sleeping with him and it will turn him off - for the long term!

If your potential mate has invited you to a party or a dance, do not disrespect him and yourself by dancing over-suggestively or with another, when it's clearly inappropriate. He'll be gone before you can say 'spontaneous combustion!'

Out to a basketball match or a ball game? Don't stroke his knees and look lovingly in his eyes, there's only one ball(s) that you should be paying attention to and that's in the game!

Joking aside, too much physical contact, especially in a public place is a turn off. If you're constantly hanging onto your date, he'll start to see you as clingy, but he'll never voice to you that he doesn't like it. Save your touches, make them infrequent and he will appreciate it more, seeing those moments as special.

When magazines educate women on how to act trashy by advising them to collect their mail from the postman in a black teddy and stilettos with captions of, 'how to capture your potential man's heart, he could be anywhere!', it's no wonder that many of today's women are slightly deranged and too 'in your face'.

When you portray an attitude of 'pick me, pick me', I'm too sexy, too funny, just plain trying too hard, then you'll send out all the wrong signals and that's of a desperate woman...and eventually he'll run...in desperation to get away!

Hold yourself with dignity and pride. If you respect yourself, then he in turn will respect you. Remember to analyse him against your criteria. If you're immediately seen to be working to be what he wants, it will reduce his respect. Don't place him on a pedestal to look down at you, he won't contribute to his potential side of the relationship and why should he when you've already given indication that you're prepared to make up for the shortfall.

You are enough, so you don't need to overcompensate for what you think you don't have or are not good enough for. Ask yourself, does this *feel* good? Does it feel like you're aligned with who you really are and how you really want to behave? Align your vibrations before meeting your date and then let the fun begin. Check how you feel emotionally and use that as your guide to keep yourself on track.

Respect your needs - your authenticity. Be classy, exude confidence and self-respect. Act like a prize, and guess what? He'll treat you as one.

Have you ever noticed the needier you appear, the faster he runs, and the more secure you appear the faster he comes? Doesn't seem fair does it?

Why is it that he runs away when you appear needy? Because you attract things to enhance your neediness and when you're secure and feeling complete and whole, you attract things to affirm this. The irony is, it feels like it should be the other way round...and that's because we've been taught the wrong way.

Ladies, don't be too much. Treat your time like gold dust. If you were to give a man a handful of gold dust and he were to let it loosely fall between his fingers... and then dust his hands nonchalantly, would you give him more?... More of your time? Think about it...

Mistake #8:
Lack Of Appreciation

This one is BIG. Another mistake that women make is failing to show appreciation. The expressing of this cost nothing and yet for a relationship is everything. Nothing will make a guy run away quicker than a woman who doesn't appreciate him.

When a guy picks you up for dinner, thank him, note the fact that he may have gone out of his way. When he drops you home after dinner, thank him again for a lovely evening and if he chose the restaurant and you had a great time, express that his choice was an excellent one. The more you appreciate a man, the more he will go out of his way to please you.

Consider this scenario: two children are before you and you give each of them a candy. One child says, 'thank you' and the other does not. To whom are you more inclined to give another? See the principle? It's human nature to want to feel appreciated and if you're looking for a long term relationship with a man, this factor alone can make or break a relationship.

If your guy buys you gifts, does little DIY jobs for you, tops up your petrol, services your car, opens those tight jam jars, each and every time: thank him!

Show him that his efforts are appreciated and never ever take things for granted or have an attitude of 'entitlement', as if that's what's expected of him. If you fail to show appreciation regularly, you'll only demotivate him and he will start to give less and less and what he does give will come from a place of obligation rather than a genuine wanting to.

Even if he gets the DIY job wrong, he's put up a shelf and it's hanging kind of wonky, smile and appreciate the thought behind the act, that it's come from a place of him wanting to please you. Tell him (tongue in cheek) how helpful he's been! Bless him!

Now, don't be afraid to compliment. Just like us women, men like to be praised. If he looks great, let him know. If he's cut his hair or changed the way he cuts his facial hair, compliment him. If he's dressed well, improved his physique in some way, compliment him. Just be genuine. However, don't lay it on too thick! A man can detect, just like us girls when you're being less than sincere.

When you show appreciation, it feels good. The more you do so, the more the Universe gives you experiences to be thankful for, that's why your partner is compelled to give. The vibe you give off attracts a like vibe.

When you truly feel gratitude, all negative thoughts are eliminated from your vibration. Use this feeling as an excuse to be who you are. Look for things to love in your date/partner and in so doing you will find the best in you. It's always good to lighten up on yourselves and others and focus on that which is good, as we all have our faults.

As women, we have got to stop trying to change our men into something to fit our own image and ideals. You can point out things you don't like in a man, in a constructive way that leaves him feeling uplifted, even inspired depending on how you choose your words. If he chooses to change his vibe, then he does so all by himself. So don't criticise him to your friends, or join ranks with that little voice in your head, belittling him; you'll only get more of it.

When you train yourself to constantly appreciate, you will see the world and others through the eyes of your inner being, your God part. You will notice that people are uplifted in your presence and that the world is beautiful. That feeling of well-being will become, if practiced, your daily vibrational default and in turn you too will be deeply appreciated by others.

Being in a vibrational state of appreciation and gratitude raises you to the frequency of love...and God is love and so you place yourself in alignment. You can start to train yourself to appreciate by beginning with yourself.

Start appreciating your attributes, your qualities, your body and health which are your blessings. After a while, like a muscle, you will train yourself into a regular pattern of thought and it will become natural to you.

What can make it hard to start, is when you're in an emotional state of feeling bad. It's a case of changing your focus, of changing your emotional state and getting out of your own way and letting your vibes incrementally move to that good feeling place. It's the absence of that alignment which makes you feel bad. So value yourself and others by showing appreciation. Praise Him often.

Mistake #9:
The Delusional Relationship

It's early on in the 'relationship', you've had a few dates and you're trying your best to keep the relationship on an even keel. You don't want the relationship to be one-sided, one person participating more than the other; you want both parties to contribute to their 50% and so you should.

However, if one of you gets too far ahead of the natural flow of the relationship and ladies, you are prone to this, you'll more than likely end up going your separate ways.

I call this *The Delusional Relationship.* Many women, after knowing a guy for only a short while, land themselves in fantasy land. Instead of seeing things as they really are, the woman is already thinking ahead, that she is **in** a relationship. Does the movie Fatal Attraction spring to mind?

The woman makes assumptions that she and her romantic interest will be spending all their weekends together, holding hands and running through fields of long grass (OK, not quite like that! but you get the picture) and that he won't be dating any other women. This is SCARY behaviour for a man and this happens when the guy hasn't even *talked* about a relationship. She then feels hurt when her expectations aren't met and she finds out that she is not his one and only.

She begins to ask things like, 'Why haven't you phoned? Who's that on the phone? Where are you? What time are you coming 'round?' She waits for him outside his workplace. She assumes plans for the weekends. The communication is unbalanced, hoping that calling, texting, emailing and checking up on him and buying him things will browbeat him into submission and *convince* him into seeing what a great prize she is.

She gives up herself and her power by no longer engaging in her usual hobbies and activities with friends. She loses herself in the relationship, over-compensating and focusing only on giving to the man; only on meeting his needs and not her own. Resentment kicks in; she feels awful and then blames him for her feelings of 'awfulness'.

Also, she seeks to govern his time and move him away from his recreational pursuits and attempts to change him by trying to make him do what he doesn't want to do. Sometimes (and really inauthentic!) she will pretend that she likes doing the same things that he does. Women, you need to maintain a sense of purpose in your lives and use your energy on controlling your own life and not his.

So why do some women do this? All in an effort to please him and have him see what a great person she is and to have him reciprocate. When a woman pursues a man like this, believe me, he will turn into Forest Gump and keep on running and running and unlike Forest, never stop! He may even change his identity, so that he can't be found.

Relax! Can you see how crazy this is???

When a woman sets down terms and conditions too early in a relationship, expressing that she's only interested in looking for a marriage partner to have a few kids with because her body clock is ticking... Woooo, hold the horses!

OOPS! Too late he's already bolted the barn!

This is not a good basis to form a relationship as every relationship has a unique connection and if you don't allow it to develop in a natural way, then you stop its natural progress and you will have turned the guy off BIG TIME. Remember at the start it's about sharing values and learning about one another, having fun and then reaching a point where you both feel the same way for the consideration of something more serious.

Think about it. You approach a guy and you don't even know him, you haven't even given yourself the chance to establish if he's a great guy or if he's a jerk, or if he's any good for you. Do you know if he meets your needs before you start setting down rules?

Enjoy the natural flow of the relationship without terms and conditions, firmly set your boundaries that serve you and give yourself a chance to receive rather than doing all the giving.

When a man gives to a woman he cares about, it gives him pleasure as he's acting out his masculine role. You've got to give a man space to be a man. Add this together with genuine and expressed appreciation on your part, and that's all he needs. Remember: appreciation to a man is what affection and reassurance are to a woman.

When you're at that vibrational point of alignment, you believe that things always work out well for you. So there is no need to rush or to force things. This belief will allow you to relax and to remain calm and composed throughout your dating/relationship experience.

Women who are relaxed and understand this flow and show that they're in no rush to get into a marriage and have the 2.5 kids are the ones that have men coming back again and again. Why? Because being around them is fun, men feel relaxed and can be themselves, enjoying the relationship at a natural pace.

Women that try to control relationships are really at heart, simply frightened. They don't feel safe. They think they're not enough and often these women attract to them men who are losers or men who are not ready. If somehow they attract a good man, this type of woman will sabotage the relationship because deep down she doesn't feel worthy.

At the end of the day, just as you cannot re-write the past, you cannot read the future. You do not know the outcome, so let go of those reins and stop trying to steer and direct the relationship. Go with the flow. Release control and live in the moment.

Mistake #10:
The 17 Miscellaneous Turn-offs

Surprise! I've got a **BONUS** for you here! For the 10th Biggest Mistake, I've compiled a list of 17 miscellaneous turn-offs as revealed by my survey of men! I didn't want to leave them out as all feedback is beneficial. It covers a variety of comments that men say turn them off - they don't come under a general consensus, as what' good for the goose is not necessarily good for the gander. For example, take women smoking, some men mind, others don't. It's dependent on the individual.

Some of these mistakes will be obvious to you but to others not. As a man is unlikely to voice these things to you when dating, you should be particularly mindful when going through the list, whilst identifying something that you do; so you can, in your awareness, choose better.

1. 'I really don't like when a woman meets with me at a restaurant or bar and she's nonchalant about being late, as if it's nothing. It makes me feel like my effort is unappreciated.'

2. 'You're sitting across a table at dinner and she's on the phone constantly; that's a turn-off. I understand people have emergencies but that's just plain bad manners.'

3. 'I once had a date; she constantly played with the acne on her face, erhh, big turn off! I made my excuses and left early.'

4. 'There was this one woman, so classy looking, except she would sneeze and then use that same hand to reach out and touch my hand or my face, gross!'

5. 'I hate when women chew gum and make loud smacking noises.'

6. 'There is nothing worse than a woman that uses profane language, every second word out of her mouth is 'f' this or 'f' that! Go learn some vocabulary.'

7. 'Women that gossip.'

8. 'This is a big one for me, women that are into dog/cat kissing and then they want to kiss me! That's just nasty!'

9. 'I think it's so unfeminine when women drink beer out of a pint glass or drink beer out of a can!'

10. 'I don't like it when women smoke, the smell on their breath and their clothes, I find it repulsive!'

11. 'I don't like it when a woman is materialistic; she's able to tell me the exact model of my watch, to my designer shirt to the kind of car I drive; to me that shouts high maintenance.'

12. 'Lack of personal grooming - hygiene, dry skin - clearly not moisturised, bad teeth ....and an instant turn off... bad breath!'

13. 'Can't take jealous women! One day we're both watching TV and an attractive woman appeared on the screen, all of a sudden, I swear to God, she started screaming, 'you're watching her, I saw you looking at her!' For goodness sake, she was on the TV!'

14. 'I think it's so unladylike for a woman to get drunk when she's out and make a total prat of herself; nothing wrong with getting a little tipsy or merry in safe company but drunk and out of it, that's a big turn off!'

15. 'When a woman lets me get away with things, that I know any self-respecting woman wouldn't, it makes me lose respect for her.'

16. 'I had a great date with this beautiful woman, conversation great, laughter, when I dropped her home, she invited me in. I was eager to do so but when I saw how untidy and dirty her home was, I was so repelled, I made my excuses and left. She lived like a pig!'

17. 'Her voice was so loud, she just seemed to always be hollering, on the phone, to her neighbours, in a restaurant, causing others to look over, she just seemed so uncouth, no tact, never spoke quietly or demurely, very unladylike.'

3
New Dating Vibes!

Dating For Fun:
Get Your Attitude On!

No doubt you found it thought-provoking looking at the dating mistakes. Did you identify anything that you do? Remember if you did, don't sweat it. Observe it and move on. Relationships and dating can be challenging and for some, especially those coming out of a long relationship and starting again, it can be a whole new ball game.

When we think of dating, we think 'western culture!' a series of social interactions between two people wanting to learn about each other for a romantic pairing. It may be serious or casual, committed or open, short-term or long-term. Whatever the reason, it's important for both parties to know their whys for dating. Potential couples may go out to dinner, attend parties, walks in the park and so on; all in an effort to get to know each other in a fun, casual and personal level to help them determine their compatibility and whether it's worth pursuing anything further.

Dates allow us to discover our differences and identify qualities we have in common and throughout this we can feel nervous, excitement and pleasure. It's also our goal to find out if we share the same core values and opinions, and in so doing, appreciate and celebrate in our sameness and our uniqueness!

Dating can be non-exclusive, which means one or both persons may be seeing multiple persons at once; this doesn't necessarily mean that they engage in intimacy with their dates but that they're simply exploring their options. Or it could be exclusive, where they both decide to date only each other, whilst exploring the possibility of a committed 'relationship' which includes both emotional and physical bonds.

Now, the main difference between dating and a relationship is the exclusivity factor. A relationship focuses on the couple and dating focuses on working out the suitability of a partner for a relationship.

What's great about dating is that it forces us to live outside of ourselves and to connect with others. It drives us to self-analyse and take action to grow to a new and improved version of ourselves. I remember being terribly shy as a teenager and making a decision to overcome this as I saw how harming it was in the forming and development of relationships and so I deliberately taught myself to smile in the mirror and to 'act' confident until I became the person I wanted to be. Now I get compliments on my smile all the time!

As we look at who we aspire to be, our dating also allows us to identify, by contrast, those qualities and wants we desire in our ideal mate and in this way we can also assess the man's values, spirituality, morals, social interests, family requirements and his goals. It allows us to determine if we would like to change or add anything to our perception of our ideal mate.

Preparing Your Mind-Set For Dating

As part of your preparation for your dates, line yourself up with who you are and what it is that you want. Feel confident, while visualising the thoughts of your desired outcome, i.e. it's a pleasant evening, all goes well, lots of laughter etc. It's not dissimilar to how I have prepared for job interviews in the past.

I would imagine the questions asked of the interviewer, write down the answers and then practice out loud over and over. On the day of the interview it would play out almost exactly as I'd practiced. At the time

I did not realise I was practicing visualisation and positively experiencing its powerful effect as it landed me my dream job.

Now the way to practice the thoughts of your desired outcome in advance of your dates is to focus on and experience, with your imagination, the qualities you most like about the men you've encountered. Focus by thinking, visualising' and feeling before you go to sleep. Your vivid visualisation of your outcome makes it active in your vibration and the LOA will then deliver to you a date that best matches those qualities.

When looking at the intention of the vibrations that you offer you can see that in designing and relying on the Universe's wonderful interpretation of your perfect mate and waiting in expectation of your desire, there is no need to fear that you are not enough for him, as it is you who has called him into your experience and it is he who has called you into his.

To reiterate (and hoping not to get too much into quantum physics here) at essence you are a vibrational being in a visible physical form and you are an extension to a source of greater non-physical, invisible energy that cannot cease to be, for energy can neither be created or destroyed.

This God-energy creates worlds and connects time and space, and some refer to this source of energy as a higher power, broader or greater consciousness and to some all-knowingness.

And so we know and rely on the love God has for us. God is love. Whoever lives in love lives in God, and God in them.

I, like many others, simply say God. This energy flows through you and is you. Everything that you perceive physically with your 5 senses are only vibrational interpretations but all is one energy. One God. One love. For God is love.

> *1 John 4:8 New International Version – UK*
> *Whoever does not love does not know God, because God is love. 1 John 4:8*
>
> *1 John 4:16*
> *And so we know and rely on the love God has for us. God is love. Whoever lives in love lives in God, and God in them.*

When you're in alignment with that energy source within you, you feel good, because God is pure love. When you're out of alignment with that pure energy source, you feel bad, because you have vibrated out of a range of that which is the love within you.

You have two vantage points. One is you, the physical you, and the other is the non-physical you - the inner you. Alignment is when the thoughts of the physical you match with the loving thoughts of the inner you.

There is only one you. We think only in terms of outer you and inner you in relation to our physical bodies. One energy, one love. Anything contrary to love is an illusion and is not of God. The illusion is fear, 'False Evidence Appearing Real'.

So when you're out on a date, remember alignment feels good! When you feel emotional disharmony it's an indicator that you are acting/behaving out of alignment with your inner being - who you really are and with what you really want.

What's Alignment?
The 12 O'Clock Analogy

I like to use a visual analogy. Imagine a clock face and both hands are pointing at the 12... It's 12 o'clock. The big hand represents the *inner you* always at one with source - God...and all whom God is: kindness, love, appreciation, abundance, absolute well-being. *(See supporting bible verses below)*

The little hand represents the *'worldly'* you and when the little hand is on the big hand, at 12 o'clock, you feel good, because you are now in alignment with God's love. You are vibrating at source energy.

When the little hand moves out of alignment of the big hand at 12 o'clock, negative feelings ensue. You feel 'resistance'. The further the little hand is away from the 12 o'clock, the more you are out of range of the vibration which is source... and so the more negative you feel, the more resistance you have to your good.

Your goal is to seek always to be at 12 o'clock. All your life you strive to be at 12 o'clock; this is where happiness resides, where you are in 'flow'. The 12 o'clock position is synonymous with your inner and physical (worldly) you, feeling good emotions.

When I'm experiencing all the good feelings, this in itself gives me joy knowing that I'm one with my source energy, my God and that from this place, only good feelings such as greatness and abundance reside.

So know this, when you are out of alignment with your inner you, just remind yourself you need to get back to 12 o'clock; you need to get back into flow and you do this by seeing things from a love perspective for God is with you always. You can simply start this by stopping in your tracks and feeling *appreciation*. There will always be something in every moment to appreciate and when you start doing this, you start to feel your way back to 12 o'clock.

Faith resides at 12 o'clock. For faith is to ask from a place of alignment and a place of well-being, 'knowing' you will receive that for which you are asking. This is the **LOA at its finest.**

Check out these verses:

(I have found through my spiritual journey, biblical based, LOA and indeed some scientific, that the truth taught are one and the same, just described differently and from different angles. I believe just as there are many fingers to the same wrist, there are many paths to God.)

Hebrews 11:1   King James Version
'Now faith is the substance of things hoped for, the evidence of things not seen.'

1 Corinthians 13:4-8   New International Version
4) Love is patient, love is kind. It does not envy, it does not boast, it is not proud.
5) It does not dishonour others, it is not self-seeking, it is not easily angered, it keeps no record of wrongs.
6) Love does not delight in evil but rejoices with the truth.
7) It always protects, always trusts, always hopes, always perseveres

1 John 4:8   New International Version
8) Whoever does not love does not know God, because God is love.

1 John 4:16   New International Version
16) And so we know and rely on the love God has for us. God is love. Whoever lives in love lives in God, and God in them.

Galatians 5:22   New International Version
22) But the fruit of the Spirit is love, joy, peace, forbearance, kindness, goodness, faithfulness.

Approach Dating With An Attitude Of Fun!

Approach dating with an attitude of fun and light-heartedness! Make it your intention to view dating as a series of fun opportunities to getting into alignment with whom you really are. When you adopt a care-free attitude of you can't get it wrong and you 'use' your date as stimuli to getting into that place of alignment, it feels good. In continuing to do this, you will train yourself into a pattern of appreciation which will help line you up on a regular basis with the love that is you.

Don't Make Him The One, Have Fun!

Whilst dating, don't try to make your date *'the one';* focus on and appreciate his good aspects, all the while viewing him as the yellow brick road to getting to 'the one'. With this approach, you make light of your relationships!

In you not making your date 'the one', you can now more readily set your mind for your task as 'information gatherer' to determine what you really want. Your experience of contrasts will give you clarity as to what you want, and as you give what you want focus, along the way you will draw to you what you are seeking, as your vibrations will refine and adapt to what you want. Be the feelings you want to attract and they will be reflected back at you.

This *'I'm having fun along the way to my perfect relationship'* approach takes the apprehension out of dating and you will find the whole dating scene much more satisfying.

Remember, when you're in alignment and feeling good it means you're on path to attracting the improved relationship that you desire. Whereas if you experience bad feelings on your journey you will never get to what you really want because you've allowed yourself on a path to what you don't want. You won't get to what you really want as you're now off the path... Got it?

Dating is supposed to be fun, about enjoying each moment; not, 'I'm looking for something serious'. Be fully present in the moment. As soon as you get attached to things having to be a certain way for you to be happy, then you lose the enjoyment of your 'now' moments and cut off love and joy. Joy and love are vibrational and are not attached at all. It just finds moments to appreciate now, right now, and so you can *choose* to enjoy right now. Date with no agenda except to 'practice'; enjoy and see where the yellow brick road leads you.

Now, it would be remiss of me to speak of dating and to not speak of falling in love, of feeling connected and wanting a deeper connection.

As your goal is to seek a deeper connection with another, then it's important to realise that what you're really seeking is a fuller connection with yourself, with whom you are. This is what you should continually reach for as it will in turn, allow for a fuller connection with another. The most important connection is the connection you have with your inner being, your God-energy. Be loving and kind to yourself. 'Be' what you seek in another and then watch the LOA deliver your perfect match.

'As a man changes his own nature, so does the attitude of the world change towards him. …
Ghandi'

Once you align yourself with your source and you are falling in love, it's natural that you should want your love reciprocated. We all want to feel loved. In fact we thrive on love. However, being in a place of not *needing* your love reciprocated is offering a love of the purest vibration as you are not dependent on the love of another to be happy. For you cannot control the love of another, only the love you offer.

If you could look at love from the perspective that you seek to attract moments that are meaningful, that allow you to 'grow spiritually' and have 'fun' as opposed to love being dependent and attached to someone to make you feel complete, then your experience would be far more enjoyable. After all, all things *are temporary.*

We have this desire to get to the end place and claim it as the final thing, which means *you are never satisfied where you are.* We exist in moments of time. There is no end place, everything is temporary. We're eternal beings forever growing, searching, expanding and like a circle there is no end. Look at it as you're using this moment right now as an opportunity to satisfy your life experience; that way you're always free and uninhibited.

As a vibrational being, only you get the credit or blame for what's occurring in your life. You get credit or the blame for how a man speaks to you, looks at you and interacts with you. It seems that they should be in control of that but everything that is happening in your life, you're attracting. When you understand this, you'll know your power as a vibrational woman and you'll feel so empowered... your alignment will mean joy, excitement, fun, anticipation, confidence and so much more.

It's important to remember that you alone are in control. No-one can vibrate for you. There are no guarantees in life and so there are no guarantees in love, so why seek to control love? In the words of the late Michael Jackson, 'This Is It'!

Switching Your Attitude To One That Serves You

Stories On Self Worth

We all want to put our best face forward when trying to attract the attention of a great guy, however, self-worth issues can often get in the way. These issues can cause problems and can affect our vibes a great deal. In our subconscious, we're running stories that cause us to behave in a habitual manner but can sabotage our efforts to live a fruitful life.

Having an *awareness* of your stories with love, i.e. no judging involved, will dispel the story and thus lose its hold on you. Stories that no longer serve you give rise to 'limiting beliefs' which hold you back, preventing you from knowing that you are enough. They cause you to operate from a space of fear but once confronted, disappear as if in a puff of smoke; like the illusions they really are.

Claim Your FREE Complementary Workbook
At www.shesgotthatvibe.com/workbook/

We create stories all the time, a constant internal chatter, attaching stories to events to give them meanings, all in an effort to protect ourselves, but in the long run, if left unchecked, protect us too much. So what's your story?

Many of these stories were formed long ago as little girls with pigtails and although consciously forgotten, subconsciously still control us like miniature puppets pulling at our strings. Your little girl mind created these stories, wrapping it around events in your life that were hurtful and harming but as an adult you no longer need protecting from. If you want to move forward in your love life, it's time to let go.

So you know what? You get to change the story. When you change your story, you change your results. You get to switch your story to one that is empowering and to one that best serves you.

Now below is such a story from a lady that shares how her low self-worth originated. Her story is an insightful one and describes how one's self-worth can be transformed by switching your story to one that empowers you. She tells two stories, one from her little girl perspective and the other as an adult.

I'm hoping that through reading her story you'll be prompted to explore the fears and beliefs that may have created the barriers to your authenticity. I hope her story helps you to delete and open new and empowering chapters to your life, thus changing your vibes for the better. (For privacy reasons, names have been changed)

Let's begin...

Part 1 - Little Girl Story - Noticed For The Wrong Reason

I tell my story as a fairy tale ...or maybe not so much ...
Kia

Once upon a time there was a young girl named Kia. She was 8yrs old, a sweet young girl of West Indi-an parentage with her hair in neat afro plaits or sometimes cornrowed in a variety of styles. She had a pretty, dark and smooth complexion like Cadbury's chocolates and a very shy smile.

Kia's favourite past time was to read. Boy...did Kia love to read! Even though she was the fastest runner in her class, when it came to playtime you would most often find Kia in a corner, alone, reading a book. As far back as Kia could remember she'd always loved books and at that time in her life she had a fascination for fairy-tales!

At home, you would find her stretched out behind the length of the 3-seater settee locked in her own world, as she cocooned herself, saturated in her fairy-tales. Kia must have read every single fairy-tale going. Her favourite were the ladybird books; they had wondrous imagery, books like 'The Princess and the Pea', 'Three Little Pigs' 'The Princess and the Frog', oh and the list went on! Then when she'd finished with those, she'd go onto the tales of Hans Christian Anderson, the brothers Grimm and onto another, always eagerly onto another.

Most of the tales she read were about characters out to seek their fortune and then they'd come across some sort of adversity, whether it be a troll under a bridge wanting to eat them, or a giant trying to get Jack's bones to make bread. Brave women like Rapunzel who let down her long golden hair so she could be saved, or Cinderella who endured the abuse of her step-mother and sisters or a Princess that kissed a frog! But what really made her beam inside were the happy endings, always, every time, they would end with her sighing as the prince married the princess, whisked her off to his Palace and they would live happily ever after....aaaah!

Outside of her fairy-tales, her reality was quite different. Kia was the second eldest and she eventually ended up with ten siblings. It was a large family, often noisy and crowded and so her favourite places of escape for reading were, apart from the back of the sofa, the quietness of the airing cupboard with the boiler to keep her warm or in the bathroom with her back to its locked door.

Both her parents were firm, her mother softer but her father stringent. She felt the love from her mother but not from her father. He never ever told her he loved her, in fact he would say the reverse. He never had a good thing to say. He was always angry. He would call her and her other sisters 'nasty'. He'd say things like, and she supposed he thought he was being funny, that if they ever got married that the door-bell would ring and there would be our husband saying, 'here, tek your nasty bitch'! Kia cannot remember a single word of affirmation or praise received from her father.

He would wake in the morning, get ready for work and then leave at 6am. Her mum would wake up around the same time in the morning and prepare him a packed lunch, usually of Bakes, (aka fried dumplings) that she'd cook from scratch filled with fried or scrambled egg. For Kia it was a pleasant smell as it wafted into her dark room that she occupied with 4 of her sisters.

When Dad would return in the evenings, every child would retreat from whatever they were doing and try to be quiet. If he entered the sitting room, they would eventually sneak out, one by one, just to be away from his very dark, removed and opposing presence. Kia didn't know what love was from a man, and up until that point she didn't even know she lacked it. She didn't know as a child how the lack of a father's love would affect her later in life. All she knew was life was what it was and she lived it!

Kia continued to do her thing, read. She would say, when I grow up, I'm going to be a fairy princess and then a handsome prince is going to come and ask for my hand in marriage, whisk me off to a palace and then I'll live happily ever after.

At age 11, as Kia began to develop into a princess, any dreams of feeling like one was shattered as her father began to touch her inappropriately...

She didn't tell anyone because when it was happening to her sister, and Mummy had been told, it appeared to her that no action had been taken. So what was Kia to do? Look after herself. Rely on herself. Escape from herself. Kia felt like she'd been on the run ever since. As she developed as a teenager she hid her beautiful figure under baggy clothes. She knew her figure was nice because at her Secondary school, the girls would always compliment her. The only problem was, to her it was a curse, because daddy knew it too. To top it all off her face was covered in horrible acne, she was on the run not just from her dad but from her own sense of self because she felt so awful.

You see, as she finished school and went home she had to put on her 'cloak of protection'. She didn't want Daddy touching her sensitive growing breasts again or pressing himself against her as he entered her room at night or speaking to her in a way no father should. She would feel so dirty. So she ensured as best she could that she was never left alone in the same room as him. For the early part of her teenage life she felt like she was constantly on the run. Ironically, being the fastest runner in her class couldn't save her! So she and her sister protected themselves as best they could. She tried to cover her sister's back as best she knew how, as she knew her sister had it worse.

One day her mum announced for the first time ever that she was travelling to the Caribbean. Kia was in knots with fear! It would be a wide open playing field, with mummy gone; who would she hide behind? He would have full control of the house! Kia got on her knees that night and prayed and prayed. 'God please take away this burden from me, please protect me, please...' Every night she prayed. And then one day her mum announced prior to her departure that her cousin would be staying, he was coming over from the Caribbean and he would be studying to be a doctor. He would be at the house in the time that her mum would be away. Hurray!

Never ever before had a relative stayed over. Kia knew her prayers had been answered and she knew she would be safe. Her father never ever tried to touch her in that period of time, she guessed for fear of being caught, and so it stopped. Her cousin ended up staying for about six years.

One day her dad returned to the Caribbean for good, leaving her and siblings behind with her mother when she was about 16. At this age, she did not know a father's warm and nurturing love, she just knew she envied it when she saw it on the TV. She didn't know how to handle men, how to value herself, she didn't have a father figure that showed or taught how. When it came to matters of love, all she knew was what she saw on the TV.

It was no surprise then, when in her early 20's she attracted a man in her life who physically and psychologically abused her because, even though he spoke abuse to her such as, 'you're like a toilet', she knew it was wrong. She stayed not only because it was *familiar* to her but because she'd seen her mother stick it out and so thought it was the right thing to do. She

thought she was exhibiting loyalty, no matter what. Not realising that she'd been taught through the example of her parents' 'low self-worth'.
Kia later had counselling from age 20 to 25.

Let's fast forward and listen to Kia as an adult......*in her own words....*

Part 2 - The Big Girl Story - Rent-A-Girl

When I was a little, my story, my life, was about fairy-tales and make-believe. Then I grew up and real life took hold. The life I was choosing was based on my experiences as a child. This is what followed...

For a long time I've allowed myself to be rented by guys as opposed to allowing them to purchase me. I say that because I've not committed myself to marriage or in fact accepted any requests for my hand to do so.

Why have I allowed this? 'Cause deep down I don't think I'm 'enough' or have what it takes to warrant a guy purchasing me. Simply, I don't believe I'm worth it...and the reason why I know I don't think I'm worth it is because I let them get away with crap or I fear speaking up for what I really want as I don't feel worthy or am of enough value.

So why don't I think I'm worth it? Because it was ground into me from young, from my parents, more-so from my dad than my mum (although she had a huge part to play as I mimicked her).

My dad would say things like when you get married one day the doorbell will ring and your husband will be at the door saying, 'here, take your nasty bitch'. My dad didn't treat me in a way as to instil in me self-worth, or make me believe that I'm a person of value or worthy of someone's love. He didn't treat me like his little princess.

I'm no psychologist but it stands to reason that a girl first learns how to relate to men by the example her father sets in her life, or by the main male figure; it all starts with the first man in her life. Her dad. My dad. And if he didn't make me feel precious like a jewel, how can I then feel precious to a man?

Even though on some level I know I'm precious, how can I present myself to a man when that's imprinted on my subconscious which runs my behaviour from the background? It seeks to protect me, because it equates too much attention, too much closeness as 'bad'. It's enough to make a girl run...

Even though I look in the mirror and see beauty, superficially I can see I'm worth it, so I attract men in my life who are a match to my vibe. I understand now that it was active in my vibration that I was a renter, not one for keeps. Like attracts like, so I attract renters.

New entry: I'm changing....

I feared being vulnerable. Vulnerability meant pain, so I found it hard to expose myself to men, not physically, that wasn't a problem but to show them my 'weak' side. I realise now that in exposing one's vulnerability and *not fearing the outcome*, that's where your strength is. But today I have changed my story, I'm not weak, I am strong. It takes guts to share your story. Hey I had to be strong to get through it, and I did. I have.

So anyway, I'm here today to change that lie. To form another 'story' around that event that an 11 year old created - that she's not worth it; to change it to I AM WORTH IT. That what my dad purported was a lie. I AM worthy of respect from a man. I AM worthy because I'm loyal. I AM worthy because of my positivity. I AM worthy because I'm beautiful. I AM worthy because I'm intelligent. I AM worthy because I'm kind. I AM worthy because I'm loving... I AM, I AM, I AM and I AM because GOD said so.

And all of this is available to the right man at the right price, which is his time, his loyalty, his respect, his kindness, his thoughtfulness, his gentleman-ness, his support and above all his love and because I deserve all of this I expect for him to want to PURCHASE me, not rent me. Before, I would never dare to think this. So now I know I am worthy of a diamond ring and a walk down the aisle. I am a princess!

Now I will say to women who have been through similar to what I have, it's time to step into your power and own it. Start walking around and holding your head high and living in a great new skin, get familiar with it, profess it!

Be clear about what you want and settle in it. Walk around in that new skin AND see how good it feels. I am.

Speak Your Truth

If someone asks you...what is it you want? What are your looking for? Speak your truth! For example, I'm looking to settle down now, I'm looking for that man who's going to give me the diamond ring because I'm worth it. It's as simple as that. I'm actually worth it because I know what I've got to give him and I know what I'm going to ask for in return and I'm not going to have any man rent my space anymore, so he can just walk on out when he's ready. That can't happen, it all starts with me...

And some women may say, like I did once, they've wasted years not knowing their worth, but I say you haven't. Life is a journey and your journey is your journey. Everything you got and are going to get is a reflection of who you are and you couldn't have been anything different from what you were and are now.

Any man that steps to you, let him know your price and then let him judge if he can afford you. If he can't, he WILL step and that's what you want right?... to get rid of the mis-matches? The time-wasters?

Every day I am enough....

(For exercises to help identify and eliminate limiting beliefs please download **workbook at www.shesgot-thatvibe.com**)

Special Note:

To me authenticity means when you become one with your Creator, that you acknowledge that you are a child of God and any thoughts contrary to that is an illusion. So for example if you have gone through abuse it doesn't mean that you have to shout it from the mountain-tops for all the world to hear, for all the 'illusions' to see. No. It means that you make your peace with God, you rid yourself of any resistance around that particular issue by forgiving, because when you forgive you let go of that resistance and you're allowing your good to flow to you, allowing God to flow through you, which is love. That's what authentic means. That's being real.

The bible says...

> *Mark 6:33 New International Version*
> *'seek ye first the Kingdom of God and all things will be added unto you'.*

Closing Thoughts:
She's Got That Vibe

People are accustomed to making things happen through action. Making things happen through thought is a new concept to them. It's a new way of being. But if you believe you are a physical as well as a non-physical (spiritual) being, then it makes sense that through thought, that has no physical barrier, you can attract what you want - from word to thought to feeling to vibration...to that inspired action - when all are positively aligned.

You now know The LOA responds to your every vibration matching it every time, no exception. Responding to your feelings - whether imagined in the mind or your observed reality. Vibrations have no history; it doesn't adapt to what you thought yesterday, it responds to your 'now'. This moment, right now! That's why it's so important to sustain your positive vibrations.

An awareness of self and self-knowledge is therefore at the root of your authenticity and I hope that through this book you have started a journey of what

Claim Your FREE Complementary Workbook
At www.shesgotthatvibe.com/workbook/

that looks and feels like. You're now aware of the power you've always had to change your vibrations, to serve you in a positive way. When you change your vibes for the better, any unwanted attention simply disappears.

Being authentically you, means you are being honest with yourself, owning your frailties, your vulnerabilities, weaknesses and strengths. It's about the *relationship you have with you*. Once you're true to yourself, having owned, confronted and changed your story around your limiting beliefs your life will transform, not just your relationships with men but with your work, career, lifestyle, friends and family!

As mentioned before, it doesn't mean that you have to shout and disclose your 'dirty laundry' for all the world to hear, it's about walking in integrity and shining your light in a way that's relevant and transparent to an individual(s) so as to help lead them out of the darkness and into the light. It's in your empathy with someone that they better relate to you and so are better equipped to guide them into their authenticity. That's being real. That's being authentic.

With this knowledge, now the real work begins. You see, it's not so much now that you know how to attract love but it's how to keep it. It's about sustaining the dynamics in your dating/relationships and other areas of your life by keeping your vibrations in line with what you want, which will of course change along the way.

Take care of those issues around un-forgiveness and remember you are the only person that can allow your doubts to rule you, pushing away the very things that you have asked for. So keep focussing on what you do want in thought, word, and deed and your goodness will come to you; I promise you, expanding every day as you recognise and appreciate what you have received.

So when you see something in your life that you do not want...think: how can I attract something I want if I'm not sending out a vibration that matches it? *Think* the vibration that you *want*.

I wish I could say that changing the way you manage your life and thus your dating and relationship experiences through your words and thoughts is an overnight process; old habits die hard and are always ready at a moment's notice to kick in. What I will say is, you can start immediately and it does get easier just by taking one step at a time. It does take conscious work and you will see results, sometimes instantly, depending on your level of resistance.

Be easy on yourself, implement one thing at a time, see the results and record them and then try another. So, if on one day you choose to think about focusing on attracting compliments, or whatever it is that you seek in a partner, do it! I recommend you record your findings in your workbook and/or a daily journal so you can see evidence of the LOA at work and the more you record, the more proof you will have to motivate your change.

Remember, nothing is more sexy to a man or in fact alluring to the world than a woman who comes from her true inner essence – her unique personal signature belonging to no-one else in the Universe. Powerful and deep attraction happens beyond physical appeal and surface smiles. It happens when a person senses – or resonates to the true vibes of another.

You really can harness your natural gift to change your influence over men and more importantly your life. So here's a big high five to you and let it be said of you, to the woman who walks in her authenticity, 'She's Got *That* Vibe'!

Namaste!
(The divine in me, bows to the divine in you)

Remember to claim your FREE workbook
that accompanies
this book at **www.shesgotthatvibe.com/workbook/**

Our Deepest Fear

By Marianne Williamson

Our deepest fear is not that we are inadequate.
Our deepest fear is that we are powerful beyond measure.
It is our light, not our darkness
That most frightens us.
We ask ourselves
Who am I to be brilliant, gorgeous, talented, fabulous?
Actually, who are you not to be?
You are a child of God.
Your playing small
Does not serve the world.
There's nothing enlightened about shrinking
So that other people won't feel insecure around you.
We are all meant to shine,
As children do.
We were born to make manifest
The glory of God that is within us.
It's not just in some of us;
It's in everyone.
And as we let our own light shine,
We unconsciously give other people permission
to do the same.
As we're liberated from our own fear,
Our presence automatically liberates others.

Note: This inspiring quote on our deepest fear is taken from Marianne Williamson's inspiring book *A Return to Love*

Valerie A. Campbell

As a serial entrepreneur and life enthusiast, Valerie A. Campbell has learned to manage her relationships through her spirituality, trials, errors and experience (both positive and not so much). With an innate desire to give back and empower other women, she has authored the recently released Book "She's Got That Vibe: How To Attract Your Boo By Being Authentically You!"

This how-to book for women describes how a woman can attract her perfect match by managing the vibes she sends out to potential mates and by learning from "The Top 10 Mistakes Women Make that Turn Men Off"; as somewhat humorously presented in this book.

By absorbing Valerie's narrative, women will understand how to send off vibes true to her intentions, how to get what she wants by becoming a deliberate thinker and how to let go of being stuck in anyone's opinion of her. Most importantly, she will learn how to develop her own ideals through being strong, clear and true to herself. "She's Got That Vibe" helps a woman understand that she never has to chase a man and that by her authentic overall presence - thoughts, words and posture; she will attract the right man.

Valerie A. Campbell was born in London to parents of West Indian origin. As the second eldest of 11 children, she learned responsibility from an early age. Because her strict parents looked down upon free expression, she never learned ways on how to interact with men from either of her parents, only from what she saw on TV! At age 18 she set up her first business selling jeans and t-shirts, sourced from her travels around the world from England to Venezuela to St Lucia and New York. These experiences increased her confidence enormously.

From there, Valerie worked in the London Council - Refuse Collection Service for 10 years. As the only female manager in a 120 male-dominated environment, she learned, from friendly talks with her 'boys' as she fondly calls them, the inner workings of the male mind, as well as the mistakes women keep making. She also studied personal development from such leaders as Earl Nightingale, Bob Proctor, Esther & Jerry Hicks and Michael Losier. Business authors - Robert Kiyosaki, Napoleon Hill, Dan Kennedy, Zig Ziggler and many others. She is a prolific reader who continually seeks to improve herself!

Valerie's spiritual growth through the word of God plus studying the power of the mind and the laws of attraction for most of her life—as well as founding her own Internet Marketing consultancy and a limited partnership company has left her greatly empowered to continue her spiritual journey and to inspire women to fulfill their spirit and destiny.

Contact Details:

Valerie A. Campbell

E: campbell_valerie@yahoo.co.uk

F: www.facebook.com/shesgotthatvibebook

P: www.pinterest.com/shesgotthatvibe/

T: www.twitter.com/shesgotvibe/

B: www.valerieacampbell.com

W: www.shesgotthatvibe.com